Contemporary Perspectives on Corporate Marketing

Corporate marketing and corporate communications are topics that have grown in scholarly and practical importance in these last decades. Fields such as branding, marketing communications and public relations have all contributed to this boost.

Whilst there is a large amount of literature on each of these disciplines, there is little systematic development from the perspective of corporate marketing and corporate communication studies, although these two have the most to contribute to how companies manage their brands, images and corporate identities in the twenty-first century. This book seeks to redress this balance and provide insights, via case studies or histories, on issues such as nation branding, managing multiple corporate identities during mergers and acquisitions and establishing a company's CSR and green image.

Scholars from various disciplines within the fields of public relations, branding, marketing and corporate identity have come together in *Contemporary Perspectives on Corporate Marketing* to offer the latest approaches and studies in these areas. As such, it will become a platform for developments in the field and serve as a respected reference resource for corporate marketing and corporate communication studies.

John M. T. Balmer is Director of the Marketing Research Group and Professor of Corporate Marketing at Brunel Business School, UK and quondam Professor of Corporate Brand/Identity Management at Bradford School of Management, UK.

Laura Illia is Assistant Professor and Academic Director of the Master in Corporate Communication at IE University, Madrid, Spain. She investigated and taught at the University of Cambridge, London School of Economics and the University of Lugano, Switzerland, where she received her PhD.

Almudena González del Valle Brena is Lecturer and Researcher (communications and digital society) at Universidad Internacional de la Rioja, Spain and Online Lecturer at IEP in Madrid. She has investigated and taught at IE University, Spain and other private universities in Spain and the UK. She received her PhD from the University of Westminster, UK.

Routledge interpretive marketing research
Edited by Stephen Brown
University of Ulster, Northern Ireland

Recent years have witnessed an 'interpretive turn' in marketing and consumer research. Methodologies from the humanities are taking their place alongside those drawn from the traditional social sciences.

Qualitative and literary modes of marketing discourse are growing in popularity. Art and aesthetics are increasingly firing the marketing imagination.

This series brings together the most innovative work in the burgeoning interpretive marketing research tradition. It ranges across the methodological spectrum from grounded theory to personal introspection, covers all aspects of the postmodern marketing 'mix', from advertising to product development, and embraces marketing's principal sub-disciplines.

Contemporary Perspectives on Corporate Marketing

Contemplating corporate branding, marketing and communications in the twenty-first century

Edited by
John M. T. Balmer, Laura Illia and
Almudena González del Valle Brena

Routledge
Taylor & Francis Group

LONDON AND NEW YORK

First published 2013
by Routledge
2 Park Square, Milton Park, Abingdon, Oxon OX14 4RN

Simultaneously published in the USA and Canada
by Routledge
711 Third Avenue, New York, NY 10017

Routledge is an imprint of the Taylor & Francis Group, an informa business

British Library Cataloguing in Publication Data
A catalogue record for this book is available from the British Library

Library of Congress Cataloging in Publication Data
Contemporary perspectives on corporate marketing : contemplating corporate
branding, marketing and comminications in the 21st century / edited by John
M.T. Balmer, Laura Illia and Almudena González del Valle Brena.
pages cm. – (Routledge interpretive marketing research)
Includes bibliographical references and index.
1. Corporate image. 2. Corporate culture. 3. Communication in organizations.
4. Branding (Marketing) 5. Corporations. I. Balmer, John M.T.

HD59.2.C65 2013
658.8–dc23
2013001761

ISBN: 978-0-415-66209-3 (hbk)
ISBN: 978-0-203-07270-7 (ebk)

Typeset in Times New Roman
by Deer Park Productions

Printed and bound in the United States of America by Publishers Graphics,
LLC on sustainably sourced paper.

Contents

Illustrations

Tables

Figures

x   *Illustrations*

Boxes

Notes on contributors

John M.T. Balmer is Director of the Marketing Research Group; Professor of Corporate Marketing at Brunel Business School and quondam Professor of Corporate Brand/Identity Management at Bradford School of Management. Previously he was Professor of Corporate Identity at the same institution. At Strathclyde Business School, Glasgow, he was Founder/Director of the International Centre for Corporate Identity Studies. Professor Balmer has written numerous landmark articles on the above areas in leading journals including *California Management Review, European Journal of Marketing, Long Range Planning, Journal of Business Ethics*, the *British Journal of Management* and *International Studies of Management and Organisations*. Since 1997 he has served as guest editor for over 16 special editions of academic journals on corporate marketing/identity and corporate brand management related concerns. He is the Founder, Chairman and Conference Organiser at ICIG (International Corporate Identity Group).

With Professor Stephen A. Greyser (Harvard Business School) he co-authored the seminal text *Revealing the Corporation* (Routledge, 2003). He has worked with a variety of organisations on research projects in corporate marketing, including the BBC, WPP Group, and the Royal Family of Sweden. He conceived and developed the MBA, MSc, and BA (Honours) electives in corporate identity/corporate branding and corporate marketing at Strathclyde Business School and at Bradford School of Management and has also run executive-level MBA electives for organisations such as the BBC, and Emirates Airways. He was the first director of the landmark MSc in Corporate Brand Management at Brunel Business School and is the founding Chairman of the Advisory Board of Experts vis-à-vis the MSc in Corporate Brand Management.

Tim Oliver Brexendorf is Assistant Professor of Consumer Goods Marketing and Head of the Henkel Center for Consumer Goods. Before taking up his position at WHU, Dr Brexendorf was a project director in a marketing consultancy spin-off from the St Gallen University, as well as a research assistant at the Center for Competence in Brand Management, a part of the Institute of Marketing and Retail at St Gallen University (today the Research Centre for

Customer Insight). There he completed his doctorate with his dissertation 'Brand Loyalty through Personal Communication – A Dyadic Analysis of Vendor–Customer Interactions on the Example of BMW'. Before his scientific career he was the e-Commerce Manager for Dialog Marketing for a joint venture by Otto Group and OBI, as well as the Junior Category Manager ECR for OBI. He earned his undergraduate degree in economics at the Carl von Ossietzky University in Oldenburg. Dr Brexendorf's research interests in the area of marketing are focused on issues of brand management, especially brand strategies, brand positioning, and interactive and employee-centric brand management. In the area of controlling he will study issues in marketing control, specifically brand control, in more detail.

Ying Fan is an Associate Lecturer at Queen Mary University of London. With more than 25 years of experience in academia, Dr Fan has taught at ten institutions including Durham, Brunel and Aston. He has been a visiting professor at Grenoble Graduate Business School in France since 2007. Fan is the author of over 80 publications on marketing and international business topics. His research work has been internationally recognised and cited more than 1,000 times, according to Google Scholar. Fan's current research relates to nation branding and nation image management. He is particularly interested in two areas: the interplay between corporate brands and country image, and the wide social impact of branding.

Almudena González del Valle Brena is Researcher and Lecturer online, UNIR (Universidad Internacional de la Rioja, Spain) and Instituto Europeo de Posgrado, Spain.

She has lectured in Media Policy, Advertising Management and Corporate Communication at IE University (ES). Her current research focuses on how issues of social responsibility and corporate identity are involved in organisational management. Dr González del Valle Brena's other main research is in public policy in the media and advertising within the European Union. She has a wide teaching experience in the marketing, communications and advertising policy areas in different Spanish universities and has undertaken consultancy for the Advertising Association (GB) in the area.

Stephen A. Greyser is the Richard P. Chapman Professor of Business Administration (Marketing/Communications) Emeritus at Harvard Business School. Professor Greyser specialises in brand marketing, corporate communications, reputation, and the business of sports. He is a graduate of Harvard College and HBS (MBA, DBA), where he has been active in research and teaching since 1958. He is responsible for 16 books, numerous journal articles, and over 300 published HBS case studies. He created Harvard's Corporate Communications course and its Business of Sports course. He has co-authored articles on monarchies as corporate brands and co-created the 'heritage brands' concept.

Professor Greyser is a former Editorial Board chairman of the *Harvard Business Review*, and past executive director of the Marketing Science Institute; he is a past president of the American Academy of Advertising and an elected Academy Fellow for career contributions to the field. His numerous awards include the Institute for Public Relations 'lifetime contributions' award in corporate communications and the American Marketing Association's 2010 Sports Marketing lifetime achievement award. He is an Honorary Fellow of London's Brunel University, where he is a Visiting Professor. He has served on numerous corporate and non-profit boards, and was national vice chairman of PBS, the US public television system.

Laura Illia is Professor in Corporate Communication at IE University and Academic Director of the Master in Corporate Communication at the same University (ES). Her current research focuses on how issues of organisational identity, social responsibility, corporate communication and branding are involved in organisational management and change. She has been doing research at the University of Cambridge (UK), London School of Economics and Political Science (UK) and University of Lugano (CH). Her works are published in journals like *MIT Sloan Management Review, British Journal of Management, Journal of Business Research, Journal of Applied Behavioral Science, Corporate Reputation Review, Corporate Communications: An International Journal, Journal of Public Relations Research* and others. She currently serves on the Editorial Boards of *Corporate Reputation Review* and *Corporate Communications: An International Journal*. In addition to her academic engagements she collaborates with Cotting Consulting International, as special coach for media, branding and image strategies.

Emanuele Invernizzi is Professor of Corporate Communication and Public Relations Management at IULM University of Milan, Italy, where he is Director of the Institute of Economics and Marketing and Director of the Executive Master in Public Relations. His main scientific contributions are ten books and several articles on strategic public relations and on organisational and entrepreneurial communication published in American, European and Italian scientific journals in the last years. He is a past President of EUPRERA (European Public Relations Education and Research Association).

Joachim Kernstock is Head of the centre of competence for brand management in St Gallen, Switzerland. He is an experienced corporate brand strategy advisor. He works with leading Swiss and European corporations and also with SMEs. He has published leading works about corporate brand management and brand behaviour in Germany and international journals. He lectures at the University of St Gallen and at the Zeppelin University Friedrichshafen. Before this engagement he was responsible for the Lufthansa corporate marketing and brand portfolio. Since 2012 he has been co-editor of the *Journal of Brand Management*.

Francesco Lurati is a Professor of corporate communication at the Faculty of communication sciences of the University of Lugano (Università della Svizzera italiana, USI), Switzerland, where he is also the academic director of both the Executive Master of Science in Communications Management (Executive MScom) programme and the full-time MS programme in Corporate Communication. He is the vice-director of the Institute of Marketing and Communication Management and the vice-dean of the Faculty. He performs research in the field of corporate communication, in particular, its impact on corporate strategy, and in the areas of organisational identity, corporate reputation and social responsibility. He was educated as an economist and received his doctoral degree from the University of Fribourg, Switzerland. He has also held positions in the public and private sectors, and regularly does consulting in the field of communications management.

Simone Mariconda is a PhD student at the faculty of communication sciences of the University of Lugano (Università della Svizzera italiana, USI), Switzerland, where he is also working as a research and teaching assistant. His primary research interest is the understanding of the dynamics related to organisational reputation and its stability over time. Other research interests include organisational identity and culture.

Belén Rodríguez-Cánovas is Associate Marketing Professor at ICADE, Universidad Pontificia Comillas. She is an economist, statistician and PhD candidate in Business Administration. She has worked as Senior Brand Manager at Kimberly-Clark, L'Oréal and Bosch. After gaining international experience in Eastern Europe in the real estate industry, she joined her family-run company as OTC Commercial Manager in the pharmaceutical industry. She combines this professional position with teaching and academic research at IE Business School and ICADE Comillas. Her main areas of interest are brand equity, private labels and generics, applications of statistics in the marketing field and CSR communication.

Stefania Romenti is Assistant Professor in Corporate Communication and Strategic Public Relations at IULM University, Milan, Italy. Dr Romenti has written and co-written over 25 international publications in communication management and public relations. She serves as a reviewer of several international peer-review journals and international conferences. She is Vice-Director of the Executive Master in Public Relations Management at IULM University and a member of the European Public Relations Education and Research Association (EUPRERA).

Gabriela Sinai has a master's degree in Marketing Management from Erasmus University; she also has a bachelor's degree in International Business Administration from the Rotterdam School of Management.

Helen Stuart is a Senior Lecturer in marketing. An experienced lecturer, having worked at three Australian universities over a career spanning four decades, she has taught marketing units at university level, mainly in the areas of consumer behaviour, marketing research, strategic marketing, marketing communication, retail marketing, marketing management, and corporate brand management.

Helen has published a number of journal articles in the area of corporate identity and corporate branding over the past 18 years and completed her PhD on this topic. She has presented her research at many international and national conferences. Her research continues to focus on corporate identity and includes an interest in sustainability in organisations. Her article was chosen as a Highly Commended Award Winner at the Literati Network Awards for Excellence 2012.

Johan van Rekom is Assistant Professor at the Department of Marketing Management at the Rotterdam School of Management at the Erasmus University in Rotterdam, the Netherlands, where he also received his PhD. His research interests include brand essence – in particular the role brand essence plays in positioning and repositioning of brands – organisational identity, the effects of organisational identity on the motivation of organisation members, as well as cognitive structures at the individual and at the organisational level.

Acknowledgements

We would like to thank Begoña González Cuesta, Dean of IE School of Communication (IE University) for her support during the ICIG conference. We are also grateful to reviewers commenting on the chapters during the review process of the conference and the editing of the book. Special thanks go to Craig Carroll, Wim Elving, Klement Podnar, and Shaun Powell.

Preface

This anthology is seemingly without parallel since it affords students and practitioners a fascinating, state-of-the-art, and highly accessible compendium of current scholarship and practice relating to the strategic fields of corporate marketing and communication. Drawing on diverse disciplinary and theoretical perspectives the book is international in scope and benefits from scholarly contributions from many renowned academic authorities from Britain, Continental Europe, the Commonwealth and North America. Adopting an explicit stakeholder stance and mindful of the saliency of Corporate Social Responsibility, this collection, in effect, bridges some of the gaps that sometimes characterise the extant literature. Materially informed by the corporate marketing perspective, account therefore is given to the strategic importance of corporate identity, branding, communication, and reputation not only as critical constructs. Moreover, these corporate-level constructs are viewed as being vital parts of a gestalt: a gestalt which is meaningfully informed by a corporate marketing philosophy.

The utility of this compendium is threefold in that it gives managers – along with MBA, Masters and more advanced undergraduate students – the much sought-after 'know-how' in terms of comprehending the strategic significance of corporate marketing and communication. In addition, it furnishes them with management tools and techniques that are not only expedient but valuable too. Finally, the practical utility of these contributions is unequivocally reinforced with the inclusion of case histories which inform every chapter and thus provide a cornucopia of institutional insights that aid understanding and learning.

The genesis of this anthology is to be found in the 14th International Corporate Identity Group (ICIG) Symposium held in 2011 at IE University Spain – one of Spain's foremost centres of management and communication – at the University's heritage campus in Segovia). Jointly organised by Dr Laura Illia and Professor John M.T. Balmer, the 14th ICIG symposium had the theme: Identity, Identification and the Management of Change. Founded by John Balmer – then a lecturer and erstwhile doctoral student at Strathclyde Business School, Scotland – in 1994, the ICIG was formally launched in the House of Lords, London in 1995. The ICIG has the aim of furthering academic and practitioner understanding of corporate identity theory and management from sundry disciplinary and national perspectives. The ICIG has been highly instrumental in furthering our comprehension of corporate identity, corporate communication, corporate branding and of course corporate marketing via numerous special editions of academic and managerial journals that date back to the 1990s. This collection very much mirrors the ICIG philosophy including the ICIG's emphasis on disseminating contemporary and cutting-edge scholarship in the area. Of course, since the mid 1990s our discernment of corporate identity has acquired breadth and depth and today corporate identity is very much viewed as a central construct in the corporate marketing and corporate communication domains.

In broader contexts, we note that scholars and practitioners within corporate marketing, communication and Public Relations – among other fields – have deepened our comprehension of the territory. However, whilst there is a large literature on each one of these domains a somewhat narrow and, at times, a parochial perspective occasionally characterises scholarly and managerial perspectives on the territory. However, we feel there is considerable merit in adopting a broad – albeit panoptic – perspective that takes account of different disciplinary perspectives and is mindful of the importance of corporate identity, corporate brands, corporate reputations and corporate communication and their pronounced interrelationships and material importance in corporate marketing contexts.

The structure and content of the book is as follows with the first three chapters providing the reader with a conceptual overview of the discipline of corporate marketing and corporate communication and a case illustration of how the brand is managed from the inside out.

Chapter 1 (John M. T. Balmer) provides a discussion and general introduction of the nature and strategic relevance of the concept of organisational and corporate marketing: a distinct branch of marketing identified and promulgated by him. To complement this conceptual discussion, Chapter 2 (Laura Illia and Stephen. A. Greyser) debates how corporate communication is a strategic discipline managing the corporate persona. In addition, Chapter 3 (Almudena González del Valle Brena) highlights the importance of internal communication and employees for managing organisations nowadays, and the importance of internal communication in supporting a corporate brand.

The following two chapters focus on corporate brands and multiple corporate identities per se and provide illuminating insights from Asia and Europe. Chapter 4 (Ying Fan) discusses the nation branding of the People's Republic of China, and Chapter 5 (Tim O. Brexendorf and Joachim Kernstock) deliberates on the multiple corporate identities – and their significance – as found within a prominent Swiss retailer.

An understanding of how brands and corporate identities can be managed in times of change is the unifying theme of the following two chapters. Chapter 6 (Emanuele Invernizzi and Stefania Romenti) discusses the above making reference to the Italian company Pastificio Rana and Chapter 7 (Helen Stuart and Belén Rodríguez Cánovas) focuses on – and details the significance of – employee and entrepreneurial (relational-oriented) perspectives relating to corporate brand and identity management.

The two concluding chapters outline the saliency of corporate social responsibility and reputation management in corporate marketing and communications contexts. Chapter 8 (Johan van Rekom and Gabriela Sinai) is a stimulating case history focussing on the Dutch detergent brand Omo, and Chapter 9 (Simone Mariconda and Francesco Lurati) focuses on two Swiss companies – the public service Swiss Post and the reinsurance company Swiss Re – and details how stakeholders' cognition and familiarity are conjoined with corporate reputation management.

Finally, it is our aspiration that the academic advances and practical insights contained within the covers of this book will meaningfully advance the reader's discernment of corporate marketing and communication. This has been realised through the practical and case history insights and via the diverse empirical, theoretical, conceptual and philosophical perspectives contained herein. We thank our academic colleagues for their insightful contributions to this compendium: not only are their chapters testimony to their sterling scholarship relating to corporate marketing and corporate communication but also they materially reflect the advances made within the field. The appeal and consequence of this book is a tribute to their work and to our ongoing collaboration and celebrates the best traditions of the ICIG and academic collegiality and sensibility.

John M.T. Balmer
Laura Illia
Almudena González del Valle Brena

.

1 Organisational marketing

Its nature and strategic significance

John M. T. Balmer

Introduction

Organisational marketing ('corporate marketing') is an increasingly significant strand of thought in management and marketing. It is an approach that is of critical importance in that it sheds light on, and therefore has the potential to reveal in much greater depth than, arguably, has hitherto been the case, the modern organisation. It can also guide managers and organisational members alike.

Organisational marketing, unlike a good deal, but not all, of extant marketing thought has an explicit corporate/corporate brand and stakeholder focus. As with earlier marketing iterations it is informed by multiple disciplinary perspectives and their attendant constructs and can be seen as an organisational-wide philosophy which is reflected in a shared corporate culture. Also, it represents a new, supplementary perspective in terms of the strategic management of organisations.

Moreover, and to expand, the adoption of an organisational marketing logic has the potential to guide managers, not only senior managers but also organisational members, in serving customers and other stakeholders in the context of the institution's mission and articles of incorporation (an organisation's juridical identity in other words). It was back in the late 1990s that I first outlined the efficacy and what I regarded would be the long-term significance of this new marketing approach (Balmer 1998).

An organisational marketing logic is an extension of the original, customer-focussed marketing orientation in that it takes account of not only the critical importance of meeting the organisation's mission so that there is mutual benefit to customers/other stakeholders but, of course, the organisation too. Importantly, organisational marketing represents an institutional-wide philosophy that is grounded in the institution's culture. It takes account of ethical/CSR concerns and the temporal dimension vis-à-vis stakeholders.

It is also a management approach – albeit a strategic management approach – which requires senior managers and strategic planners to take cognisance of multiple corporate-level constructs (such as corporate identity, branding, communication and image); to ensure that they are meaningfully and, importantly, dynamically aligned with the aim of winning and maintaining customers along with maintaining, too, the support of other stakeholders which can be critical in terms of ensuring financial support and in terms of attracting employees, etc. As such, one criterion for a successful corporate marketing orientation is the degree to which there is a strong and positive identification with the organisation – among not only employees and customers but other stakeholders and organisations as well. Of course, positive identification must translate into action in terms of buying products and services, supplying the company, investing in the firm and working for and staying with the organisation, etc. To reiterate, organisational marketing does not operate in a vacuum. This is because corporate marketing – as a philosophy and as an approach to strategic management – can provide one effective means through which an organisation's mission and objectives, as set out in its charter or articles of association, can be achieved.

Whilst organisational marketing is in certain regards similar to stakeholder management there is a difference in that accord is giving to the temporal dimension. As such, as well as showing regard for stakeholders of today and tomorrow, the organisational marketing approach acknowledges that the contributions made by stakeholders in earlier times can often be meaningful: consider mutual organisations, for instance (building societies, co-operative entities). Although it would be perverse in strategic terms to give undue regard to the past there can, all the same, be merit in such an approach and there may, perhaps too, be a moral case for the same. Consider, for instance, those mutual financial institutions whose memberships have been passed on from one generation to another but, in the wake of financial deregulation in the 1980s, became public limited companies. Consider former British building societies such as Abbey National, Bradford and Bingley, and Halifax Building Societies. Whilst it took generations to build up these entities, by changing their status to public limited companies (PLCs), overnight, investors and borrowers of the societies' financial products and who were, for the main, treated as members of the society, became shareholders and were able to sell their shares and derive financial gain – something that earlier members were not allowed to do.

In more holistic terms, corporate marketing is both a modus vivendi (a way of living) and a modus operandi (a way of working) which, as a philosophy and strategic management approach, has applicability to contemporary organisations of whatever size, nationality, or, indeed, hue. Over recent years we have witnessed a growth of interest and this is reflected in those articles which have, in whole or in part, focussed on corporate marketing, namely: Aspara and Tikkanen (2011), Karaosmanoglu *et al* (2011), Podnar *et al* (2011), Powell (2011), and Illia and Balmer (2012).

In bringing this introductory section to a close, it is worth recapitulating some of the key tenets of the domain. As such, it can be said that organisational marketing – as a powerful, albeit additional, strategic perspective and institutional-wide philosophy –affords an additional lens through which scholars and managers can more fully comprehend organisations and their interfaces with stakeholders from both multiple identity as well as from strategic perspectives. It is an integrative and multidisciplinary approach that is meaningfully informed by the key, corporate-level constructs of corporate identity, corporate brand identity, corporate communication, corporate image and reputation which typically inform our comprehension of the territory from marketing, communication and from strategic perspectives. This being said, organisational marketing also takes account of member identification with an institution which is an abiding concern of organisational behaviourists and which, in recent times, has been broadened by marketing scholars and others to accommodate customers and other stakeholders.

The chapter's focus

This chapter provides an overview of the organisational/corporate marketing field and explicates the bases of the domain and outlines the corporate marketing rationale along with its strategic importance. Organisational marketing, to me, is a natural development of marketing thought. Organisational marketing – although qualitatively different from the traditional customer-focussed product and services marketing logics – complements and advances earlier marketing approaches. As such, it is an approach that is inextricably linked to earlier marketing orientations in their various manifestations and should be viewed as augmenting these earlier, albeit powerful and practical, approaches.

Corporate marketing represents more of an evolution – albeit a somewhat radical evolution – and not a revolution of marketing thought. So, just as extant marketing approaches (marketing orientations and logics) have highlighted the importance of products/product brand, services/service brand in meeting customers wants and needs (including business-to-business interactions) in commercial and not-for-profit entities, etc. since the late 1990s (Balmer 1998), organisations per se (their identities and corporate brands) and stakeholders and not just customers have also been shown to be highly significant. This is because organisations – including their corporate identities, corporate brands, along with their philosophies and culture and CSR activities – can be central in terms of meeting the wants or needs of not only customers but also stakeholders.

However, there are other dimensions to be considered. This is because organisational marketing is also inextricably linked to the corporate communication, corporate image/reputation, and corporate branding, etc. domains. Importantly too it is informed by identity-based views of the firm perspective and it's meaningfully informed by multiple identity perspectives. As such corporate marketing/ organisational marketing is an important means by which institutions can profitably meet their legal, economic, societal, and other objectives. This chapter on organisational marketing is primarily informed by my own research and scholarship in the area dating back to the 1990s.

Corporate marketing or organisational marketing?

Whilst I use both the organisational marketing and corporate marketing terms in this chapter it is important – as a brief but important aside – to explain something of their links and respective meanings.

For the main, there is no contradiction in using the two terms interchangeably in management, marketing and organisational contexts. However, there are differences between the two terms.

Organisational marketing

Organisational marketing, in comparison to its sister construct of corporate marketing, is narrower in scope in that it explicitly refers to institutions per se – of whatever shape or form – and as such does not refer to cities, countries and so on.

Corporate marketing

Corporate marketing is a construct that has a broader applicability in that it applies not only to organisations but also to entities of whatever shape or form, and this includes countries, territories and regions, along with state, civic and religious entities (monarchies, cities –including the ancient City of London – dioceses and of course universities). The term corporate – as many of us will probably recall from our days as MBA students – comes from the Italian expression to break bread together and, thus, it is a salient reminder that corporate refers to any collective group. In law, the notion of the corporation is a very ancient one indeed and referred to towns and later universities as bodies corporate. In identity terms this was a significant development since it recognised that institutions had an actual existence and – as with an individual – could buy and sell property and could sue and be sued.

Of course, among marketing, branding, communications and image/reputation scholars it has been the *corporate*, rather than the *organisational* label that predominates in terms of the labels by which they categorise their research, scholarship and teaching, namely: *corporate* identity, *corporate* brands, *corporate* communications, *corporate* image, *corporate* reputation, etc. The titles of their books and masters courses also include the word corporate too, such as MSc courses in *Corporate* Brand Management and *Corporate* Communication. As such, it seems entirely logical that the umbrella of *corporate* marketing should be used.

The above can be compared with scholars from organisational behaviour and related disciplines who eschew reference to all things corporate in labelling the constructs which have come from and which primarily inform their work relating to identity and image. Their preferred word is *organisational*, namely *organisational* identity, *organisational* identification, *organisational* image, etc.

Problems and inconsistencies

Curiously, some scholars in marketing and communications – even though they make wide reference to corporate brands, images, reputations and communications – entirely avoid reference to *corporate identity* but refer to organisational identity instead (this somewhat radically warps the historiography of the field and accords the organisational behaviour literature – important thought it is – hegemony and ignores the work of marketing, communications scholars and practitioners in the field. This has caused, and continues to cause, unnecessary confusion and represents a distorted narrative. For their part, organisational behaviourists such as Hatch and Schultz (2001) make reference to corporate brands rather than organisational brands which (from their organisational behaviour stance) would appear to be entirely illogical in light of their disciplinary associations.

Links with marketing/communications and organisational behaviour

So, from the above we can clearly infer that whereas the *corporate label* tends to refer to and identify the work of marketing, communications and strategists in the domain, the *organisational label* tends to identify the work emanating from organisational behaviourists and analogous areas of scholarship. However, what should be a clear logic can be put aside for a variety of reasons. There is another, quite important, consideration in terms of usage of both these terms.

The British and North American divide explained

Whereas in the UK, and in parts of the Commonwealth and in Continental Europe where there is still some familiarity with the historical roots of the corporation as a term and a greater realisation that the word corporate can be used in a wide sense, this is not – from experience – the situation which exists in a good deal of North America. There, among many managers and management scholars, the word corporate for the main refers to a narrower institution form – the *for profit* enterprise (joint stock companies) and therefore is seen not to apply to other institutional forms. This being said, I have no doubt that lawyers in the USA and Canada, where both countries' legal systems (with the exception notably of the Canadian Province of Quebec and US State of Louisiana, where in both the Napoleonic Legal Code prevails) are derived from English law, will be all too familiar with the original and traditional meaning accorded to the word corporate. The same, for the main, cannot, alas, be said for many others.

   This short aside helps, I hope, to explain to the reader why I have accorded greater prominence to the organisational marketing construct in this chapter but I do, as will already have been apparent, also make reference to corporate marketing too. It would be a great shame if barriers of language, education and tradition should mitigate furthering the global awareness of the corporate and organisational marketing territory. It is an area that, potentially, can be of material benefit to scholars and practitioners alike. As such, I think a degree of sensitivity on the part of the English is called for. It is always better to build bridges than to break them. Indeed, the attractiveness of organisational marketing vis-à-vis corporate marketing as a construct was kindly commented upon by a number of my esteemed US colleagues very recently. As some readers may be aware, both I and Dr Powell have taken account of this in the mid 2000s on our corporate marketing and organisational marketing website where we have taken meticulous care in using and explaining both these terms. As such, although I prefer for intellectual and practical reasons making reference to corporate marketing, such a stance may have the unwanted effect of the area being missed on the North American radar. That would be a shame and, perhaps, irresponsible too. So, as a *via media* – and very much in the British tradition – I shall compromise and use *both* constructs!

Organisational marketing: mirroring the contemporary zeitgeist

The current zeitgeist in management scholarship and practice variously stresses the strategic importance of corporate brands, corporate identities, corporate communications, corporate reputations and images – along with other corporate-level constructs. This being noted, to me it is unquestionably the case that the organisational marketing approach meaningfully links the above concerns/ constructs into a meaningful whole: a whole that is informed by a clear and transparent overarching organisational philosophy: a philosophy that can be meaningful not only to managers but to other organisational members too.

It is, alas, very much the exception rather than the rule that these corporate-level dimensions are meaningfully linked in other disciplinary canons. More often than not, and for perfectly understandable reasons, authors tend to privilege one approach over another. Moreover, there have been only a few attempts to consider these corporate-level constructs in the round so that a logical and persuasive modus operandi emerges.

Of course, individual areas such as corporate communications, corporate identity and corporate brand identity scholarship have made important, if not profound, contributions to the domain but such approaches, for all of their utility and undoubted sophistication, are necessarily restricted in scope owing to their disciplinary foundations (this is as true of marketing scholars as it is of those from other management disciplines).

There is an exception to the rule: the nascent organisational marketing/ corporate marketing domain.

Although, curiously, the area has not received much attention in North America, corporate marketing/organisational marketing has, all the same, attracted the attention of a growing number of scholars in the UK, the Commonwealth and in Continental Europe too. Arguably, marketing has been in a good – if not in a pole – position in terms of advancing the domain since, historically, marketing has marshalled theories and insights from a plethora of areas such as economics, psychology, sociology, communications, strategy, image research, jurisprudence, etc. Marshalling insights from these areas, marketing scholars and practitioners have elucidated various marketing philosophies which have guided not only organisational members but also senior managers in meeting the wants and needs of customers to the benefit of organisations in product, services, business to business, not for profit and charitable focussed entities.

Organisational marketing is very much of the same, albeit earlier, marketing traditions in terms of articulating an innovative organisational gestalt, by nurturing a contemporaneous and salient institutional philosophy and culture focussed on customers and other stakeholders and, importantly and in addition, represents an innovative – and arguably very powerful – approach to strategic management.

Organisational marketing: what is it?

The delineating attributes of organisational marketing can be characterised in terms of an organisational-wide philosophy and culture. As such, the values and ethos of firms having an organisational marketing orientation manifest themselves in terms of having an explicit institutional, stakeholder, and societal orientation: a culture and philosophy which, significantly, is meaningfully informed by a CSR/Ethical ethos (Balmer 2011).

Organisational marketing is, of course, one of several distinct marketing paradigms: other marketing paradigms respectively focus on goods and services and, for the main, focus on customers. Organisational marketing is different in that it focusses on organisations (on corporate identities) and, in addition, on corporate brands. Moreover, although a marketing orientation recognises the critical importance in having an organisational-wide customer orientation this approach is broadened in the corporate marketing field so as to encompass a stakeholder orientation in addition. Organisational marketing is also very much informed by the notion of identity-based views of the firm and – this is becoming decidedly important – identity-based views of corporate brands (Balmer 2008). The significance of corporate brand identities in this regard cannot and should not be underestimated (Balmer 1998, 2001a, 2009, 2011).

To elaborate further, in order for this organisational-wide philosophy to be actualised it has to be reflected in the organisation's culture. Moreover, organisational marketing should be at the core of a firm's strategic deliberations. Table 1.1 outlines what for me are the defining characteristics of organisational marketing and Box 1.1 provides an earlier definition of corporate marketing.

Organisational marketing and organisational members: their respective roles

In comprehending the organisational marketing domain it is important to understand the role senior managers and personnel have within it.

Senior managers

The role of senior managers: critical role in fostering an organisational marketing orientation (in terms of philosophy and culture) and in marshalling organisational marketing insight and data in terms of informing corporate strategy. Senior executives are the ultimate guardians of organisational marketing. Senior managers do, of course, have specific roles in terms of setting corporate communications and in terms of corporate image and reputation research, etc.

8   *John M. T. Balmer*

Table 1.1 Organisational marketing – defining characteristics

An explicit corporate – rather than product or service – orientation (as such both the corporate identity and the corporate brand are of critical importance)
A philosophy which has a customer/stakeholder, CSR/Ethical and societal *foci* and ethos
Enacted via a corporate-wide culture
A philosophy that – in temporal terms – is concerned not merely with the present and prospective future but is mindful of the past (for instance the inheritance bequeathed to an organisation by its owners, founders, etc.)
Informed by a corporate-level gestalt (appreciates the meaningful contributions to organisational marketing by comprehending key corporate-level marketing constructs such as corporate communication, corporate identity, corporate brands, etc.)
Powerfully revealed and apprised by adopting an identity-based view of the firm and by, in addition, adopting an identity-based view of corporate brands (and draws on theories relating to the above)
Multidisciplinary in scope

Organisational members

Personnel are of critical importance in that they have day-to-day responsibility for the delivery of an organisational marketing logic. This is because a company's corporate marketing orientation needs to be lived, enacted, and communicated via everything an institution says, makes and does and in this regard organisation members are key. Following on from this, there needs to be a supporting organisational marketing culture within an institution in order for a corporate marketing ethos to be realised.

Organisational marketing: antecedents

In a 1998 article in the *Journal of Marketing Management* entitled: 'Corporate Identity and the Advent of Corporate Marketing' (Balmer 1998) we can see the genesis of organisational marketing/corporate marketing. From the outset, corporate marketing was viewed as a distinct strand of marketing thought, strategy and practice. Since then I have further elaborated the nature, management importance and strategic significance of the domain in other articles, books and chapters (namely Balmer 1998, 2012b, 2009, 2011; Balmer and Greyser 2003, 2006; Illia and Balmer 2012).

Also back in 1998 I argued (Balmer 1998) that the logical destination of practitioner and academic interest in the corporate-level constructs of corporate image, corporate communication, corporate identity, corporate reputation, and corporate brands was the ascendancy of a new umbrella marketing paradigm: corporate marketing (organisational marketing can be viewed as an analogous term).

Box 1.1 Organisational marketing ('corporate marketing') – a definition

Corporate marketing (organisational marketing) is a customer, stakeholder, societal and CSR/Ethical-focussed philosophy enacted via an organisational-wide orientation and culture. A corporate marketing rationale complements the goods and services logic. It is informed by identity-based views of the firm: this is a perspective which accords importance to corporate identities and corporate brands. The latter provide distinctive platforms from which multilateral, organisational and stakeholder/societal relationships are fostered to all-round advantage.

Whilst its primary focus in on mutually advantageous multilateral organisational and customer/stakeholder partnership of the present and future, a corporate marketing logic also has sensitivity to the institution's inheritance. The corporate marketing (organisational marketing) orientation is also mindful of its corporate responsibilities in societal, ethical and in CSR terms. All employees share responsibility for the corporate marketing orientation but senior managers and the CEO in particular have ultimate stewardship of the corporate marketing (organisational marketing) orientation. The espoused benefits of a corporate marketing logic include the establishment of ongoing and bilateral positive organisational/customer-stakeholder relationships; the establishment and maintenance of trust, and the acquisition of meaningful and positive corporate reputations; the creation of shareholder and/or shareholder value via the establishment of strong, salient and appealing corporate brands; institutional saliency in its markets (corporate survival and profitability) and the licence to operate in terms of the organisation's societal, ethical and CSR by virtue of the organisation's responsibilities and sensibilities in terms of the aforementioned.

Source: Balmer 2011: 1345–6

Note: Organisational marketing is narrower in scope than corporate marketing in that it applies to institutional entities (corporate marketing can apply, for instance, to cities and other non-institutional entities).

For me, this new marketing domain was characterised by having an explicit institutional and stakeholder-focussed orientation. As such, there is a concern with multiple exchange relationships with multiple stakeholder groups and networks, both internally and externally (for example with and between owners, managers and employees). Another key feature is the importance accorded to the temporal dimension with there being fidelity not only to present relationships but also to those of the past and those prospective relationships of the future.

Organisational marketing and its development from goods, services and relational logics

The antecedents of organisational marketing are varied (see Balmer 1998, 2001a; Balmer and Greyser 2006; Balmer 2011) and organisational marketing represents a distinct new marketing logic (Balmer 2011). Taking an historical perspective, organisational marketing can variously be viewed as a logical development of earlier marketing logics including a product/goods logic (McKitterick 1957; Levitt 1960), services logic (Vargo and Lusch 2004) and the relational logic (Coviello and Brodie 1998; Gronroos 1997).

Organisational marketing. A logical development of integrative endeavour: sensory integration, design integration, communications integration, brand integration, identity integration and organisational marketing integration

Arguably, organisational marketing is a logical denouement of various integrative endeavours at the corporate level. These diverse integrative concerns include integrated design, integrated communication, etc. and all of these may be seen to have meaningfully informed the organisational marketing sphere (Balmer 2009: 569–70). As such, with the passage of time various attempts have been made in terms of integration and these include sensory integration, design integration, communications integration, brand integration and identity integration which may also be seen to have betokened what to me is the inexorable rise of an organisational marketing logic (Balmer 2011). Of importance, too, is how organisational marketing has powerfully been informed by identity-based views of the firm/corporate brands perspectives (Balmer 2008, 2009, 2011).

Comparing traditional marketing with corporate marketing/ organisational marketing

Table 1.2 details the similarities and differences vis-à-vis the above approaches.

Operationalising organisational marketing: corporate marketing mixes

Since 1998 onwards I have introduced a number of corporate marketing mixes (frameworks). My aim has been to capture – as well as communicate – the key dimensions that inform the organisational marketing domain. Having a clear organisational marketing mix helps to clarify and operationalise the domain and therefore may be seen to have a value for practitioners, scholars and preceptors alike. As such, I have attempted to follow in the footsteps of McCarthy (1960) and Borden (1965) vis-à-vis the marketing mix. This being said, unlike McCarthy's mix, I have pointed out (Balmer 2011) that my various iterations of the corporate marketing mixes are broader in scope; require a radical reconfiguration

Table 1.2 Indicative comparisons between organisational marketing and 'traditional' marketing approaches

Focus	Organisational marketing	Traditional marketing
Orientation	Customer and stakeholder orientation focussed	Customer orientation
Delivery	Corporate identity (the firm's traits) and the corporate brand (brand promise)	Goods and services and product and services brands
Temporal (time) foci	Focus on the present, future and the past	Focus on the present and future
Exchange relationships	Multilateral and multi beneficial exchange relationships with all stakeholders and the society and over time	Bilateral – and mutually beneficial – exchange relationships with consumers
CSR/Ethical concerns	Central	Optional
Culture and philosophy	The existence of a strong organisational marketing culture and philosophy are critical	The existence of a strong marketing culture and philosophy are critical
Management	CEO and the management board	The Director of Marketing/ marketing directorate
Responsibility	All staff	All staff
Coordinating function	At the corporate level (corporate strategy)	At the directorate and also the corporate level (marketing strategy and corporate strategy)

of the traditional marketing mix; and are underpinned by broader distinct disciplinary traditions than with earlier marketing approaches.

To date, three organisational marketing mixes inform the domain. From my teaching of the area, along with feedback from academic colleagues in other business schools, it would appear that each mix has its merits and strengths in terms of breadth, depth, memory, and utility. For instance, my 10Ps of corporate marketing seems to be well liked by marketing students who are familiar with other marketing mixes and especially the classic 4P marketing mix (product, price, place and promotion).

The first marketing mix: the 10Ps of corporate marketing (Balmer 1998 and 2006)

The initial corporate marketing mix develops and expands the traditional and famous four Ps of marketing so that it has applicability to corporate entities and corporate brands. The mix comprises Philosophy, Personality, People, Product,

Price, Place, Promotion, Performance, Perception and Positioning (Balmer 1998). In 2006 he added a further P in order to capture the corporate brand identity: that of Promise (see Balmer in Balmer and Greyser 2006).

The second marketing mix: the HE²ADS² model (Balmer 2001a)

In my second marketing mix (Balmer 2001a) there was something of a departure in that the mix dimensions were simplified and the mix – in order to aid the memory of its elements – formed the acronym HE²ADS² and comprised seven elements. The dimensions can be explained as follows: what an organisation Has (soft and hard assets which add value and distinctiveness) and Expresses (corporate communication); being mindful of the Environment (the political, economic, social, technological, ethical and legal environmental concerns); taking account of stakeholder Affinities (identification to the firm/corporate brand – informed by social identity theory; also being mindful of what the organisation Does (the organisation's corporate identity); along with showing sensitivity in terms of how the entity is Seen (corporate reputation and image) and adopting an overtly Stakeholder orientation (informed by stakeholder theory perspectives).

The corporate marketing Cs (Balmer 2006 and 2009)

Arguably, it has been the corporate marketing Cs (Balmer in Balmer and Greyser 2006) which has been the most popular of the marketing mixes. As I have recently explained each corporate marketing mix dimension (each C) is inextricably linked with the others. As such a change to one C element will impact on other dimensions of this mix.

To recapitulate, this mix focuses on corporate marketing Cs rather than corporate marketing Ps and my original mix accommodates the following dimensions:

- Character (what the organisation indubitably is)
- Communication (what the entity says it is)
- Constituencies (whom the organisation seeks to serve)
- Covenant (what is promised and expected from the corporate brand)
- Conceptualisations (what the firm is seen to be)
- Culture (what we feel we are)

Three years later in 2009 (Balmer 2009) I went on to include two additional dimensions and these are:

- Context (the wider environmental concerns which must be taken account of)
- Custodianship (senior management stewardship of the corporate marketing ethos and this also embraces the notion that the corporate marketing logic is the responsibility of all employees)

Organisational marketing and corporate identity/corporate brand alignments

Another line of scholarship within marketing/corporate marketing dating back to the 1990s (Balmer and Soenen 1999; Balmer 2001b; Balmer and Greyser 2002; Balmer *et al*. 2009) has stressed the need to ensure that an organisation's rationale and purpose are reflected in terms of ensuring that its activities are meaningful and are evidenced in what it does, and how it does it (corporate identity). It also notes that corporate identity can be shaped by management vision (desired identity) and by an organisation's strategic intent, focussing on a given period of time (ideal identity). This approach, therefore, is informed by the view that corporate identity should be dynamically and broadly aligned with an organisation's corporate communications (communicated identity), and should be calibrated with customer and stakeholder perception.

Identity-based views of the firm/identity-based views of corporate brands and organisational marketing

Another, critically important, way in which organisational marketing can be comprehended is by scrutinising the domain through multiple identity perspectives and, more specifically, through identity-based views of the firm and via identity-based views of corporate brands (Balmer 1998). At a simple level, the identity-based view of the firm/identity-based view of the corporate brand perspectives draw on extant theories and scholarship relating to corporate identity (the defining traits of an organisation/corporate brand); corporate identification (the way an organisation/corporate brand identifies itself to the world and to its stakeholders via communication: this marshals corporate communication theories); organisational identification (the degree and manner by which individuals and groups associate themselves with an organisation/corporate brand: this is informed by social identity theory); cultural identification (the degree and manner by which individuals and groups associate themselves with an organisation's/ with a corporate brand's culture: this can also be viewed as a variant of social identity theory). The identity-based perspectives are illustrated in Table 1.3.

The identity-based view of the firm/identity-based view of corporate brands approach –informed by the precepts of organisational marketing – has led to the so-called ACID Test model which represents a diagnostic framework which highlights identity misalignments: misalignments which can be potentially hazardous to organisations (Balmer 2001b, 2012a, 2012b; Balmer and Greyser 2003; Balmer *et al*. 2009). The approach is informed by the view that multiple identities should be *dynamically aligned* with each other: this represents a centrifugal approach to identity alignment. Recently the importance of culture and the corporate brand per se has been accorded greater prominence in the ACID Test framework (Balmer 2005, 2012a, 2012b), as has the efficacy of temporal alignment.

The very latest version of the framework adopts an explicit identity-based view of the corporate brand approach, informed by the view that multiple identities

Table 1.3 Explaining identity-based views of the firm/identity-based views of corporate brands perspectives

	Organisational focus	The corporate brand focus (a corporate brand can, it should be remembered, be shared by multiple entities)
Identity *OF* the firm/ identity of the corporate brand	The defining and differentiating traits of an organisation	The defining and differentiating traits of a corporate brand
Identification *FROM* the firm/identification from the corporate brand	The defining and differentiating traits of an organisation that are communicated to the world and to customers and other stakeholders	The defining and differentiating traits of a corporate brand that are communicated to the world and to customers and other stakeholders
Identification *TO* the firm/identification to the corporate brand	The degree to which individuals and groups are attracted by and/or are closely aligned with the firm in terms of their values and aspirations	The degree to which individuals and groups are attracted by and/or are closely aligned with the corporate brand in terms of their values and aspirations
Identification *WITH* a firm's culture/ identification with a corporate brand culture	The degree to which individuals and groups are attracted by and/or are closely aligned with the firm's corporate culture in terms of their values and aspirations	The degree to which individuals and groups are attracted by and/or are closely aligned with a corporate brand culture in terms of their values and aspirations

Source: based on Balmer 2008

should be dynamically calibrated with the corporate brand identity and covenant (Balmer 2012a, 2012b). See Table 1.4 for this.

Of interest, too, is the widely cited work of the US/Danish organisational behaviour scholars Hatch and Schultz (2001) which was published in the *Harvard Business Review*. Their work, focussing on the corporate brand, has a similar, albeit a very much narrower, *raison d'être* with the scholars arguing that only vision, culture and image should be in alignment. In contrast my ACID Test approach has for a considerable time now taken into account identity, the corporate brand, constituencies and, importantly, corporate communication. See Balmer (2012a, 2012b) for the latest version of the ACID Test.

Organisational marketing: theoretical perspectives and foundations

Organisational marketing is underpinned – as with traditional marketing – by very many theoretical perspectives. These include identity-based views of the

Table 1.4 The latest version of the ACID Test comprises the following identity types

Actual identity	based on the corporate identity: the defining and differentiating traits of an organisation
Communicated identity	based on corporate communications: how the organisation identifies and defines itself to the outside world and to its customers and other stakeholders
Conceived identity	based on corporate image and reputation: how the organisation is perceived by individuals/stakeholder groups
Covenanted identity	based on the corporate brand identity: the brand promise 'covenant' that is associated with a brand name and or *marque*
Cultural identity	based on the firm's values and the ways individuals and groups within the firm make sense of an entity
Ideal identity	based on strategic planning: the optimum positioning and identity of an organisation in a given time frame
Desired identity	based on the CEO's/senior management's vision for an organisation in a given time frame

Source: Balmer 2005, 2012a, 2012b

firm/identity-based views of corporate brands theories (Balmer 2008) – the notion that multiple identities inhabit and meaningfully inform the organisation. Social identity theory (Tajfel and Turner 1979) – which has been marshalled by organisational marketing scholars to explain an individual/a group's degree of affinity with a corporate brand or corporation – is also highly significant. Moreover, the significance of organisational marketing's stakeholder orientation means that stakeholder theory is highly salient (Freeman 1984), as is commitment-trust theory (Morgan and Hunt 1994). The social construction of identity is also significant (Goffman 1959) and can be marshalled in organisational marketing contexts. Of relevance too is company–customer identification theory (Bhattacharya and Sen 2003); this can be broadened to encompass other stakeholder groups; institutional theory (Powell and DiMaggio 1991) – since corporate marketing has an explicit institutional focus – and core competencies theory (Prahalad and Hamel 1990). The economic theory of the resource-based view of the firm is also highly salient (Grant 1991), as is the business concept theory (Norman 1977), which is closely aligned to coporate identity as it relates to an organisation's distinctive traits.

Organisational marketing developments: ethical organisational marketing

The corporate marketing/organisational marketing logic can also be adapted to institutions having an explicit ethical/CSR remit and this has given rise to the notion of Ethical Corporate Marketing/The Ethical Corporate Identity and the Ethical Corporate Brand (Balmer *et al*. 2011, Balmer 2012a). However, communicating an ethical corporate marketing logic is different from having an ethical corporate marketing logic and where the latter does not conform to the former there can be difficulties as the BP Deepwater Horizon tragedy revealed (Balmer 2010, 2012a).

The British Petroleum and British Airways case examples, detailed below, provide two salient case examples which will further highlight the importance of corporate marketing.

British Airways' organisational marketing logic and management

Arguably, there are few airlines whose legacy and proud provenance can match that of British Airways (BA). The carrier's roots are twofold. First, dating back to 1924 when four small UK-based airlines merged to become what was then known as Imperial Airways (very much reflecting the zeitgeist of the period). Second, Britain's airline presence in Continental Europe and South America was realised in 1935 with the establishment of British Airways. With nationalisation in 1939 the BA brand disappeared but was to re-emerge in 1974 when the successor airlines of Imperial Airways and British Airways (The British Overseas Air Corporation –'BOAC'– and British European Airways –'BEA'–) merged to form an airline that, once again, was to be known as British Airways (BA from now on).

From this period to 2000, BA had to tackle various identity alignment issues – and what in the context of this chapter we would surely also characterise as organisational marketing problems too. The longitudinal case study revealed that issues relating to corporate branding, identity, communications, reputation, culture and stakeholders were not only critical concerns but, moreover, were interrelated. As such, taking a broad multiple identity perspective (as per the ACID Test framework) along with a corporate marketing perspective was efficacious.

Let me detail one, celebrated, corporate marketing problem faced by BA in the late 1990s. In what was surely one of the most audacious repositioning exercises of any legacy airline brand, BA, in 1996, decided to position itself as an international rather than a British airline. As part of this new strategic orientation for the airline, BA was no longer to have one visual identity which had a pronounced British character but approximately 50 global symbols which were to be found most strikingly on the tailfins of BA planes. The strategy was a catastrophic flop and showed how a narrow communications and perceptions based strategy is dangerous when issues of corporate identity, culture, corporate branding and the wider stakeholder environment are not taken account of (as per an organisational marketing logic). What went wrong? From a stakeholder perspective, by downplaying BA's British heritage the airline alienated its British customers, upset the British Government and also upset its travelling public; many customers – especially those from North America and the Commonwealth – actually liked and appreciated the British nature, service and orientation of the former BA. Moreover, although there had been a change of face – in terms of formal corporate communications and visual identity – the culture of the airline was steadfastly British. As such there was a major misalignment here, too. Also, the airline failed to take account of its brand inheritance and reputation as a solidly British airline. Lastly, taking a temporal perspective, account should have been given to former stakeholders and organisational founders who had invested their time and energies in building up the airline as not merely a symbol of a proud company but – as with many legacy airlines – as an icon of the state. By downplaying BA's British roots, BA's senior managers were, unwittingly perhaps, undermining British identity. Some companies have, it should be remembered, not only a corporate role but a national and cultural one too. As I was told by the late Lord Marshall (then Chairman of BA):

> As it turned out, the airline had gone too far, too fast for its key stakeholders – customers, shareholders, employees – and the British public. The change was too drastic and in the view of many weakened the strength of our brand. There was also the perception that the proud heritage of British Airways was being swept under a carpet of modernisation.
>
> (Lord Marshall, cited in Balmer 2012a: 18)

For further information on the British Airways case see Balmer (2012a: 6–33) and Balmer *et al.* (2009: 6–23).

BP and the Deepwater Horizon catastrophe

In the late 1990s and early 2000s what was then known as British Petroleum acquired a number of US-based petroleum concerns such as Arco and Amoco and this changed the very nature of the corporation. Whilst, formerly, it had been a decidedly British organisation it was now a truly Anglo-American entity with the firm having almost as many US shareholders as British. The new situation caused BP to rethink its branding and communications strategy and, guided by the US-based branding consultancy Landor, among others, the company was no longer to be known as British Petroleum but simply as bp (the lower case is intended since the firm wished to convey a less corporate and more caring ethos). A strikingly new logo was adopted along with a new strapline. The new logo aimed to communicate the company's new green, environmentally friendly and socially responsible ethos and agenda (bp communicated that it was committed to renewable sources of energy). The visual identity made great use of green and pastel colours and included an image of the sun (emphasising renewable energy). What of the new strapline? Well, bp was now shorthand for a new corporate motto, namely: 'Beyond Petroleum'.

From a corporate marketing and identity alignment perspective there was a huge problem here – something that we pointed out in 2002 (Balmer and Greyser 2002). What bp was communicating to its stakeholders and to its customers regarding renewable sources of energy and a concern for the environment seemed to be some distance away from the firm's identity and the reality of oil exploration, extraction, processing, distribution and retailing. It's quite difficult – perhaps impossible – for an oil firm to be truly green. That being said, the motivation of Lord Browne, the CEO of bp, was undeniably sincere and well intentioned but the efficacy of having a branding platform built on the above was, and is, highly questionable. Moreover, the culture within the organisation and the desire to keep down costs and keep up company dividends also sat unhappily with the above. The explosion on the Deepwater Horizon caused extensive environmental damage in the Gulf of Mexico (there was also loss of life), which has, by some, been attributed to bp's (and its business-to-business customers' too) poor safety standards. Again, too much attention was focussed on putting a positive communications spin on the organisation without taking full account of the firm's identity, ethos and mode of operation. The traditional daredevil culture of bp did not sit happily at all with the new branding strategy and the shortcomings of this stance came to the fore at the time of the Deepwater Horizon catastrophe. The bp case raises another, very interesting, point and it is this. The degree to which organisations can be Ethical/CSR orientated will vary according to type, modes of operation and business focus. This does not mean that such firms should not take account of the above, or of stakeholders, only that the degree to which they can, or should, do so will vary. bp's green and ethical stance is a prime example of this. What they were doing, although quite small in the big scheme of things, was ahead of its time vis-à-vis oil companies and credit is due to the company for this. What was an error, however, was to make the above concerns the major focus of the firm's corporate communications policies. Again, this case illustrates the efficacy of adopting a holistic corporate marketing approach. Ironically, in the months leading up to the tragedy a public relations spokesman for bp, commenting on the oil giant's brand positioning, said the following: 'Our aspirations remain absolutely unchanged: no accidents, no harm to people, and no damage to the environment' (Randall 2010).

For further information on the bp case see Balmer (2012a: 6–33); Balmer (2010: 97–104); Balmer *et al.* (2011: 1–14); Balmer and Greyser (2002: 72–86).

Conclusions

This chapter has explained the nature, history, models and theories relating to corporate marketing/organisational marketing. It is my hope that I have communicated the strength and value in scrutinising organisations via the lens of organisational marketing. To me, it is a perspective that can have real value for scholars, managers and practitioners working in the domain. Moreover, it provides a common umbrella under which I believe all those – including academics, preceptors, managers and consultants, and of course students –whose interests reside in corporate identity, communications, branding, along with corporate image and reputations, scholars and others can comfortably stand without any sacrifice of their disciplinary identities and allegiances on their part. Finally, the dictum that the whole is very much greater than the sum of its parts is something that especially applies to organisational marketing.

References

Aspara, T. and Tikkanen, H. (2011) 'Corporate marketing in the stock market: the impact of company identification on individuals' investment behaviour', *European Journal of Marketing* 45(9–10): 1446–69.

Balmer, J. M. T. (1998) 'Corporate identity and the advent of corporate marketing', *Journal of Marketing Management* 14(8): 963–96.

—— (2001a) 'Corporate identity, corporate branding and corporate marketing: seeing through the fog', *European Journal of Marketing* 35(3–4): 248–91.

—— (2001b) 'From the Pentagon: a new identity framework', *Corporate Reputation Review* 4(1): 11–22.

—— (2005) 'Corporate brands: a strategic management framework', *Bradford University School of Management Working Paper Series*, 05-43.

—— (2008) 'Identity-based view of the corporation: insights from corporate identity, organisational identity, social identity, visual identity and corporate image', *European Journal of Marketing* 42(9–10): 879–906.

—— (2009) 'Corporate marketing: apocalypse, advent and epiphany', *Management Decision* 47(4): 544–72.

—— (2010) 'The BP Deepwater Horizon Debacle and corporate brand exuberance', *Journal of Brand Management* 18(2): 97–104.

—— (2011) 'Corporate marketing myopia and the inexorable rise of a corporate marketing logic: perspectives from identity-based views of the firm', *European Journal of Marketing* 45(9–10): 1329–52.

—— (2012a) 'Corporate brand management imperatives: custodianship, credibility and calibration', *California Management Review* 54(3): 1–28.

—— (2012b) 'Strategic corporate brand alignment: Perspectives from identity based views of corporate brands', *European Journal of Marketing* 46(7–8): 1064–92.

Balmer, J. M. T. and Soenen, G. B. (1999) 'The ACID Test of corporate identity management', *Journal of Marketing Management* 15(1–3): 69–92.

Balmer, J. M. T. and Greyser, S. A. (2002) 'Managing the multiple identities of the corporation', *California Management Review* 44(3): 72–86.

—— (2003) *Revealing the Corporation: Perspectives on Identity, Reputation, Corporate Branding and Corporate-Level Marketing*, London: Routledge.

—— (2006) 'Corporate marketing: integrating corporate identity, corporate branding, corporate communications, corporate image and corporate reputation', *European Journal of Marketing* 40(7–8): 730–41.

Balmer, J. M. T., Stuart, H. and Greyser, S. A. (2009) 'Aligning identity and strategy: Corporate branding in British Airways in the late 20th century', *California Management Review* 51(3): 6–23.

Balmer, J. M. T., Powell, S. M. and Greyser, S. A. (2011) 'Explicating ethical corporate marketing. Insights from the BP Deepwater Horizon catastrophe: the ethical brand that exploded and then imploded', *Journal of Business Ethics* 102(1): 1–14.

Bhattacharya, C. B. and Sen. S. (2003) 'Consumer-customer identification: a framework for understanding consumers' relationship with companies', *Journal of Marketing* 67(April): 76–88.

Borden, N. (1965) 'The concept of the marketing mix', in Schwartz, G. (ed.) *Science in Marketing,* New York: Wiley.

Coviello, N. E. and Brodie, R. J. (1998) 'From transaction to relationship marketing: an investigation through mutually beneficial perceptions and practices', *Journal of Strategic Management* 6(3): 171–86.

Freeman, R. E. (1984) *Strategic Management: a stakeholder approach*, Boston: Pitman.

Goffman, E. (1959) *The presentation of self in everyday life*, London: Anchor Books.

Grant, R. M. (1991) 'The resource based view of competitive advantage: implications for strategy formulation', *California Management Review* 33(3): 114–35.

Gronroos, C. (1997) 'From marketing mix to relationship marketing – towards a paradigm shift in marketing', *Management Decision* 35(4): 322–39.

Hatch, M. J. and Schultz, M. (2001) 'Are the strategic stars aligned for your corporate brand?', *Harvard Business Review* 79(2): 129–34.

Hildesbrand, D., Sen, S. and Bhattacharya, C. B. (2011) 'Corporate social responsibility: a corporate marketing perspective', *European Journal of Marketing* 45(9–10): 1353–64.

Illia, L. and Balmer, J. M. T. (2012) 'Corporate communication and corporate marketing: Their nature, histories, differences and similarities', *Corporate Communications: an international journal* 17(4): 415–33.

Karaosmanoglu, E., Bas, A. and Zhang, K. (2011) 'The role of the other customer effect in corporate marketing: its impact on corporate image and consumer-company identification', *European Journal of Marketing* 45(9–10): 1416–45.

Levitt, T. (1960) 'Marketing myopia', *Harvard Business Review*.

McCarthy, E. J. (1960) *Basic Marketing: A Managerial Approach*, Holewood, IL: Irwin.

McKitterick, J. B. (1957) 'What is the marketing concept?', in Bass, F. M. (ed.) *The Frontiers of Marketing Thought and Science*, Chicago, IL: American Marketing Association, 71–82.

Morgan, R. M. and Hunt. S. D. (1994) 'The commitment-trust theory of relationship marketing', *Journal of Marketing* 58(July): 20–38.

Norman, R. (1977) *Management for Growth*, London: John Wiley.

Podnar, K., Golob, R. and Jancic, Z. (2011) 'Identification with an organisation as a dual construct', *European Journal of Marketing* 45(9–10): 1399–1415.

Powell, S. M. (2011) 'The nexus between ethical corporate marketing, ethical corporate identity and corporate social responsibility: an internal organisational perspective', *European Journal of Marketing* 45(9–10): 1365–98.

Powell, W. and DiMaggio, P. J. (1991) *The New Institutionalism in Organizational Analysis*, Chicago: University of Chicago Press.

Prahalad, C. K. and Hamel, G. (1990) 'The core competence of the corporation', *Harvard Business Review* 68(3): 79–91.

Randall, R. (2010) 'Oil spills disaster: the guilty parties', *The Independent* (13 June): 7.

Tajfel, H. andTurner, J. C. (1979) 'An integrative theory of intergroup conflict', in Austin, W. G. and Worchel, S. (eds) *The Social Psychology of Intergroup Relations*. Monterey, CA: Brooks-Cole.

Vargo, S. L. and Lusch, R. F. (2004) 'Evolving to a new dominant logic in marketing', *Journal of Marketing* 56(January): 1–17.

2 Corporate communication and the corporate persona

Laura Illia and Stephen A. Greyser

This chapter focuses on what Illia and Bauer (2009) characterise as 'corporate persona' – namely, how organisations define themselves.[1] The concept has its roots in psychology and the organisational culture underpinning identity formation, described in a later section. The ideas manifest themselves in the corporate and organisational worlds in terms of elements such as identity, image, and reputation as well as the particular organisational culture in which they are nested and which they reflect and project. In the past decade, the study of corporate persona has concentrated on identity, notably in the work of a number of scholars who consider the company a social actor (Whetten 2006) that holds multiple identities (Balmer and Greyser 2002) and copes with its multiple identity gaps (Hatch and Shultz 2002, 2008; Balmer 2012) as well as issues of corporate marketing (Balmer and Greyser 2006; Balmer *et al.* 2009) and reputation (van Riel 1995).

The above provides a challenging setting for organisations seeking to project and shape effective impressions of their persona in a multiple-stakeholder environment. Indeed, the broadening of the relevant stakeholders is a phenomenon of the past two decades, as many companies have found that regulators and other government entities, communities near factories and offices, advocacy groups, and even the media themselves are calling for the observation and monitoring of attitudes and behaviour. These add to more traditional groups such as unions and employees, the financial community, and often the general public. In the following paragraphs, we demonstrate how corporate communication is one of the corporate functions aimed at managing this complex set of stakeholders from an identity-based view.

Corporate communication and its evolution

Corporate communication is the dominant vehicle for disseminating information and ideas intended to project an organisational persona. When most effective, such communication is based on a clear understanding of the multiple identities that combine to constitute the persona, research into the most relevant stakeholder groups' views regarding company-related issues (Illia 2003), and a sensible assessment of which (and how) organisational initiatives (policies, actions, and supporting communications programmes) are likely to affect these groups positively (Cornelissen 2011). Corporate communication also aims to manage various inter-organisational relationships with groups upon which the company is dependent (van Riel 1995; Cornelissen 2011) as well as fulfil expectations by addressing gaps between what a corporation does and what it says (Illia and Balmer 2012). Following this line of research, corporate communication plays an important role in managing not only secondary or tertiary communications projected by the company and its intermediaries such as media and activist groups, but also any of the company's primary communications – namely, corporate or staff behaviour (Balmer and Greyser 2003). Corporate communication also has an important obligation to manage the gaps between various identities of the corporate persona, which is a function that it shares with corporate-level marketing (Illia and Balmer 2012).

This tripartite role of corporate communication (i.e. managing corporate messages, corporate behaviours and any potential gap between them and the stakeholders' expectations) is the result of an evolution of the field that emerged parallel to the changes in how companies interact with audiences and think about themselves. Most notable among these is the continuing technology-driven change that affects both the speed of the communications cycle (issue–message–response) and the ability of both companies and audiences themselves to communicate broadly. Technology, the growth of social media, and the broad availability of digital platforms currently put the tools of message dissemination into the hands of virtually anyone and any group, thereby having a profound effect on the structure of corporate communications and its stakeholder-driven philosophy. If companies were previously the undisputed protagonists in a communication arena, where only mass media and other key intermediaries such as activists were operating, then today managing corporate communications means recognising that 'everyone is a publisher' of a company's related information. Managing communications about and especially defending an organisation is more complex and (as noted) occurs in faster time cycles. In such a context, social media are rarely – if ever – inactive when a company issue is tepid, let alone hot.

Yet this recent noteworthy shift towards social media and digital communication is not the primary and only change that signalled the transition of corporate communication from message-driven to a company's total communication function (Balmer and Greyser 2003). Shannon and Weaver's (1949) traditional one-way communication model (communicator–channel–audience) had already undergone a shift in the late twentieth century. Companies increasingly found that news media were less accepting of company messages as the latter were increasingly seen as 'spin' in many situations. In addition, company problems in times of organisational travail attracted high media visibility. Company and executive misbehaviour fed this trend, as much wider stages of learning about and reporting on troubles presented themselves. As a result, both the strategic and operational elements of corporate communications call for careful management. On one hand, it is essential to manage any corporate identity and corporate brand gap strategically; on the other hand, it is crucial to manage specific programmes and content elements operationally. This brought companies to

Box 2.1 Moving ahead of the traditional advertising and communication management policy

Traditional communication programmes used to emphasise implementation whereas new programmes emphasise analysis (van Riel 1995). This analysis assesses images, expectations, stories, and perceptions of a wide range of publics and stakeholders with relevant capability to take actions. In this context, auditing employees becomes a central element in aligning a company with its stakeholders (van Riel 2012) as they are considered not only human resources, but also an essential part of the corporate persona's expression. The final aim of new programmes is to achieve the optimal situation in which the company maintains very good relationships with all stakeholders. For example, an arms or tobacco manufacturer provides excellent quality for its customers, but might have to fend off a constant flow of bad news arising from attacks on its business from NGOs or public health officials who put a 'stigma' on their operations. Improving the quality of efforts will not be the solution to their problem of the corporate persona. Rather, the corporation will have to understand its stakeholders and their impact and perhaps try the route of corporate social responsibility and defend a controversial product by doing societal good in other ways.

move beyond the traditional advertising and communication management policy towards an identity-brand, and reputation-based policy.

Analysis is indispensable. However, it is also essential to recognise that the profession has changed its routines. For example, corporate communication professionals changed the way they manage media relations when news media changed their routines. Compounding the rise in direct communications between organisations and publics is the modification of the media's sourcing of stories. The use of social media and Twitter by reporters for stories and opinions (expert or not) has increased. According to *PR News* (19 October 2012 online), Chris Brooks (Hilton Worldwide) considers this significant, especially when tweets are quoted as a valid source. From an organisation's standpoint, staying in touch with the media community via online vehicles is another important aspect of the 'new corporate communications'. This complex communications environment of expanded stakeholders and multidirection communications also creates a more sophisticated setting for executives responsible for strategy and communications. Today, executives are responsible for analysing a strategic decision not only in financial or operational terms, but also in the corporate persona terms. This increases the need to educate managers in understanding the corporate environment from a communication standpoint. It has also ultimately enhanced the role of the chief communication officer, who is an important alter ego for other executives sitting on the board.

The resulting challenge is elevated by what Greyser terms 'an environment of enhanced expectations' of corporate behaviour. Several factors inhabit this environment: the diminishment of the public's institutional trust (as shown in the Edelman Trust Barometers); the increased salience of trust as a core attribute of organisations; the increased emphasis on transparency in institutional behaviour; and a growing recognition of the relevance of authenticity as a key ingredient in an organisation's make-up. In recent years, authenticity and 'the authentic enterprise' have become hallmarks of the Arthur W. Page Society, the principal American professional association of major corporate communications officers. Their 2007 and 2012 publications described and advocated for authenticity and 'building belief' in companies via authenticity. To us, a key implication is that company behaviour must support its communications – what Greyser calls the congruence of *acta et verba*. This is especially salient in times of brand crisis (Greyser 2009). The Page perspective posits that a vital role of the chief communications officer, not only as a person responsible for communications (by harnessing a range of capabilities and tools) but also as a 'curator of corporate character', is maintaining company focus on its core identity. The Page CCO-oriented approach supports our belief that it is essential to manage the corporation as a corporate persona – that is, as an individual authentically managing all its identities in use.

The corporate-person analogy

To understand how to manage the corporate persona, it is important to comprehend the theoretical underpinnings of the corporate-person analogy. Symbolic *interactionism* and the resulting impression management perspective are at the core of its genesis. The relations between the individual and collective action is a complex matter, but for the present chapter's purpose, the impression management of collectives and individuals is functionally analogous. Ideas about impression management originate in sociological traditions of social psychology (see Goffman 1959; Cooley 1902, 1956; Mead 1934). Individuals establish an identity in interactions that guides their actions and enables them to anticipate what to expect from others (Erikson 1980). It translates to organisations in terms of how people present themselves at work (Schenkler 1985; Rosenfeld, Giancalone and Riordan 2002; Tedeschi 1981) and how companies project themselves to stakeholders in the wider public (Etang 2008; van Riel 1995; van Riel and Fombrun 2007; Hatch and Schultz 2002, 2008). According to Goffman (1959), people give (intended) and give off (unintended) expressions of themselves. Expressions are signal vehicles that convey information about a person's identity, but they also offer a definition of the situation. For example, when doctors wear a white coat, clearly they are not only telling us who they are, but also making us aware of the fact that they are a doctor whom we can consult for health problems. A similar thing happens with companies. When companies build modern eco-friendly buildings, they give information on where their headquarters are as well as the idea that we will be able to count on them as an environmentally friendly actor.

The construction of a corporate persona

The analogy of how people and collective organisations give and give off expressions was suggested some time ago by Albert and Whetten (1985), who provided an influential statement on how organisations define their identity. Organisations construct their identity through 'a process of ordered inter-organisational comparisons and reflections upon them over time' (Albert and Whetten 1985: 273). Other scholars (e.g. Gioia *et al.* 2000) traced this idea directly to Cooley (1902/1956) and Goffman (1959), stressing that a company's process of identity formation is related to an image of itself, on the basis of which an organisation can change itself (i.e. the organisational collective 'I' or the 'us'). Still others (see Hatch and Schultz 2002, 2008; Jenkins 1996) traced this story to Mead (1934), thereby adding that a company's identity is based upon its culture and its image (i.e. the organisational 'I' [us] and the corporate 'me' [us]), as shown by Figure 2.1. The one stands for the internal real self, the other for the externally adapted presentation of self – the role played in a particular situation.

Like an individual who expresses an 'I' (who am I?), a company holds an 'organisational I-us' (who are we?). The 'I' and 'organisational I-us' are responses to perceptions of those who give an opinion on who we are. Individuals and collectives respond to these perceiver attitudes not directly, but through the 'me' (what am I?) (Mead 1934) and 'corporate me-us' (what are we?). Contrary to the 'I' that is autonomous, the 'corporate me' and individual 'me' are relational constructs managing relations to others. Citing Mead:

> we carry on a whole series of different relationships to different people. We are one thing to one man and another thing to another. There are parts of the self which exist only for the self in relationship to itself. We divide ourselves up in all sorts of different selves with reference to our acquaintances.
>
> (Mead 1934: 140)

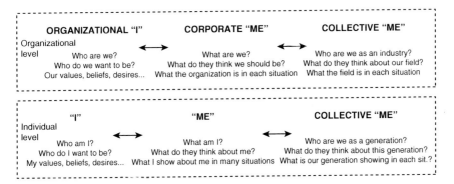

Figure 2.1 Comparing how organisations and individuals define who they are (authors' elaboration inspired by Hatch and Schultz 2002, 2008)

Linking Mead's reasoning to Goffman's, one might assert that the 'me' is a necessary part of the everyday interaction because it permits audiences to situate others' identities. The 'me' provides people with the situated identities for the specific role played out in front of a particular audience or stakeholder at a given time. The organised 'me' plays an important role. It permits individuals to juggle different expectations and construct an image accordingly, without losing the integrated identity (of the 'I-us'). The collective 'me' is the group identity that is subject to specific legitimisation and permits individuals to build their own image accordingly. For example, if an individual is a member of a specific generation, nation, or group, he/she has either a positive or negative halo effect of its image or reputation, which is mirrored internally as a reflection of how to manage his or her own behaviours.

How corporations give and give off expressions

For an individual, even more so than for a corporation, it is problematic to experience a situation where the 'I' and the 'me' are disconnected. For a company, the risk of creating false expectations arises when the identity projected is not really a part of the organisation. To avoid this situation, corporate managers must have a clear picture of the real and stable 'organisational I'; they must also manage how to respond to audiences' perception, the 'corporate me', in light of this picture. Yet it is also important to be aware of the various 'corporate me's' and be clear to which audiences they refer as well as to what extent they are touted in the 'organisational I'.

According to Gioia (1998), organisations have it easier than individuals in terms of juggling multiple images because a company can plausibly have many masks, each one being relevant to a different audience, without appearing hopelessly fragmented and schizophrenic. What for an individual borders at mental illness, the multiple personality syndrome, is for corporations a normality. However, this relative ease does not mean unproblematic. The multiple faces of a company still faces the problem of consistency. Avoiding the decoupling of the 'organisational I' and 'corporate me' requires some control over the gap between intentional communication expressed at the corporate level in terms of intended and unintentional communications given off at the organisational level, as Figure 2.2 indicates.

Field level

At the field level – namely, the level of companies who share similar identities, interactions, and institutional logics (Greenwood and Suddaby 2006: 28) – the collective 'me' embodies the grand narrative (Fiol and Romanelli 2011), which represents the symbolic communication (Lounsbury and Glynn 2001) and legitimised institutional voice (Lammers 2011) that describes what a corporation has in common with others. This identity-driven communication is operated by 'leading collective identity advocates' (Wry *et al.* 2011: 456) or central actors (Greenwood and Suddaby 2006) that mobilise grand stories which characterise

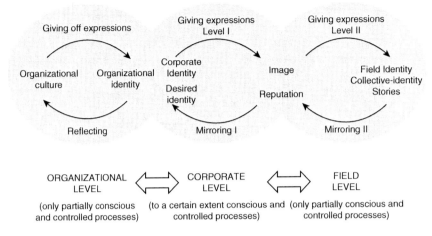

Figure 2.2 Linkages between organisational and corporate expressions (authors' elaboration inspired by Hatch and Schultz 2002, 2008)

this 'recognized area of institutional life' (DiMaggio and Powell 1983: 64–5) of a group of companies. It is crucial that the organisation be able to mirror this second level of the collective 'me' because it constitutes an important source of alignment of the company's core ideology with the institutional logics operating in its context. An example of this would be a company operating in the oil industry which needs to mirror in its operations the new legitimising corporate social responsibility standards that are typical of its industry. To manage this situation, the company needs to adapt to such standards as well as manage its corporate image as part of this specific industry.

Corporate level

At the corporate level, top managers give intended expressions about who the company is through corporate projections of identity. At certain moments, companies ought to take particular care of their corporate expressions, such as during times of rapid growth, increased competition, or monopoly disruption. Such companies usually need to position themselves in a new way to compete in the market. Competition with big competitors requires them to develop a new corporate identity, with new advertising and logos that might enable them to stick in consumers' minds. To control this situation, the company must define its identity based not only on its desired identity (i.e. the outcome of internal 'reflections'), but also on what they can see in the 'mirror' of their stakeholders' perceptions. In this way, they integrate the image of externals as a resource to develop corporate identity statements which, together with other corporate communications, give expressions of the company with the aim of forming a company's or organisation's image. Mirroring is also important during turbulent crises.

They ought to develop expressions that accommodate what images stakeholders already hold. To construe the 'corporate me', it is not enough to reflect, but it is also necessary to mirror outsiders' perceptions. Thus, it is important to be in continuous contact with stakeholders and understand how their perceptions stack up and how and why they are changing. Clearly corporate activity is only one among many factors that structure these stakeholder perceptions.

Organisational level

A company, as well as individual persons, is able to comport itself intentionally only to a certain extent. To minimise the risk arising from this lack of self-control, corporate communicators need to consider two additional factors. First, slippages of expressions of the organisation are always possible and likely. What is required is vigilance and attentive analysis of the company. The organisational identity and culture are resources for developing the corporate identity of statements, symbols, and programmes (Hatch and Schultz 2002, 2008). Corporate identity should not go against the grains of existing organisational practice. In this way, identity statements are embedded in real culture and are not 'blue sky' irrelevances discrepant from what is given. Consistency between corporate expression and impression as well as between organisational and corporate reality is important, particularly during mergers and acquisitions, as the merged company needs to reconstitute its identity more than ever. Second, the internal reflection of corporate images, the construed image within the organisation, is another location in this hall of mirrors. Members' behaviours permeate what stakeholders – customers, suppliers, media, local community – think about the company. What others think of us affects how we operate. Managers must consider the members' reflected images of the corporation arising from various sources of scattered images (Price *et al.* 2008) of what the organisation stands for. For example, the mass media, read by employees, contribute to building a corporate image independent of the strategic attempts to position the corporation intentionally (Kotler and Kotler 1998; Balmer and Greyser 2006). The image, as a social construction, is based on the interpretative resources of the audiences, and the official sources are not the only source (Christensen and Askegaard 2001).

The strategic concerns: analysing the corporate persona and measurement tools

Managing the corporate persona requires an appropriate management of various gaps and misalignment among the company's image, reputation, and identity (van Riel 1995; van Riel and Fombrun 2007; Illia and Balmer 2012). Such gaps and misalignments offer important insights as they constitute the moments of truth for the corporation (Balmer and Greyser 2002).

Let us take the example of an entrepreneur who produces eco-oriented products and tries to enter a new market. The identity-image questions facing this entrepreneur are numerous: How will our products be sustainable in terms

Table 2.1 Definitions

Field identity	Companies that share similar identities, interactions, and institutional logics	Greenwood and Suddaby 2006
	Identity-based communication is operated by leading collective identity advocates	Wry *et al.* 2011
	Institutional identity shared by organisations collectively	Glynn 2008
Image	A means for the audiences to summarise opinions about their direct experiences with a company	Berens and van Riel 2004
	A set of meanings by which an object is known and through which people describe, remember, and relate to it. It is the net result of the interaction of a person's beliefs, ideas, feelings, and impressions about an object	van Riel 1995; Dowling 1986
	A representation that affects attitudes which in turn affect behaviour. The impression it creates – consciously or unconsciously – inevitably affects people who do business with the company	Bernstein 1984
	The way a company is perceived based on a certain message at a certain point in time. It is induced through corporate communication	Cornelissen 2011
Reputation	An enduring collective representation of a firm's past behaviour	Cornelissen 2011; Fombrun *et al.* 2000
	The audience's social expectations of a company due to an indirect experience of the company	Berens and van Riel 2004
	The relatively stable, long-term, and collective overall judgments of externals about an organisation, its actions, and achievements	Fombrun 1996; Fombrun and Shanley 1990
Corporate identity	Statements on a company's personality, profile, symbols, and values. It is the mix of attributes which makes the company unique	Cornelissen 2011; Balmer and Greyser 2003
	The image of a company that it communicates to its constituents; it might or might not represent the substance of the company	Alversson 1990; Bernstein 1984
	Strategically planned, consistent, and targeted representations of the corporation emphasised through corporate symbols and logos	Olins 1989, 2008; van Riel and Balmer 1997
Desired identity	What managers desire the company to be; the professed ideal of the company	van Riel 1995; Soenen and Moingeon 2002; Balmer 2012
	The perception the managers would like members and externals to have about the company	Gioia and Chittipeddi 1991; Gioia and Thomas 1996
	A resource to build a corporate identity and represent the core ideology and envisioned future about a company	Collins and Porras 2000

(*Continued*)

Table 2.1 Continued

Organisational identity	Members' interpretations of what is most core, distinctive, and enduring in the organisation	Albert and Whetten 1985; Lerpold *et al.* 2007
	Perceptions and beliefs about what is central, distinctive, and enduring in their organisation; internal members' identities understandings (of the organisation)	Dutton *et al.* 1994; Ravasi and Schultz 2006
	Reflects what the organisation really means to different groups at different times in the organisation	Gioia *et al.* 2000
Construed external image	Members' perceptions about what outsiders think about the company	Dutton and Dukerich 1991; Dutton *et al.* 1994
	How employees think outsiders see their organisation. It comes from various sources of information, such as opinions of reference groups, word of mouth, and external company-controlled information	Smidts *et al.* 2001
Organisational culture	Basic assumptions, values, and symbols of the organisation defining how things are done	Shein 1980
	A general system of rules that governs meanings in the organisation	Smircich 1983

of image and identity? Is our eco-oriented culture in line with the expectations of the market? Can employees behave eco-compatibly? Is the eco-image of the company in line with financial market expectations? Does the company already have an eco-reputation? Might that help at all when entering the market?

The example shows that the analysis of gaps in the situation, issues, and current positioning of the company is a priority. One has to understand what this might mean for the company's current identity and image, which requires identifying any decoupling between internal and external images of the company, including the benchmarking of competitors. This also requires an extended analysis of the misalignments of field identity, reputation and image, desired identity, organisational culture and identity, and the construed image of members. Only with the result of a gap analysis among all of these elements in hand can one decide whether to maintain or adjust the positioning or determine what the consequences of any repositioning might be for the identity, image, and reputation of the company as well as how to implement all this in a communication programme.

The variety of tools and methods is too large to provide an exhaustive list here. An entire chapter could be devoted to this task. However, it will be useful for the reader to know the basic options for the analysis of corporate identity and image.

A number of typical concerns exist, such as actions of employees creating a bad image, a new positioning to be decided and communicated, lack of cohesion and

Table 2.2 Suggesting when to measure what

What and in which order	When to measure what
1. Organisational culture 2. Image 3. Organisational identity	Behaviour of employees creates bad image Lack of support during a change Negative attitude of employees Lack of 'we feeling' Issues of employees' commitment
1. Desired identity 2. Corporate identity 3. Organisational identity (in a second round when failures of expectations emerge) 4. Reputation 5. Field identity	New strategy/positioning has to be decided New strategy/positioning has to be communicated and be attractive for internals New strategy/positioning has to be communicated in a consistent way to externals Communicating the 'we feeling' Positioning creates failure of expectations Positioning creates unexpected impressions on externals Lack of legitimacy
1. Field identity 2. Reputation and image 3. Organisational identity 4. Desired identity	New strategy and position has to be decided Bad image and reputation Negative attitude of external audiences Lack of external audiences' support during a crisis External expectations do not support a position Externals are important sources for the company's image Lack of legitimacy The organisation wants to impress/express externals with a specific personality or image

we-feeling in the organisation, a positioning creating false expectations, and issues of image and reputation. Choosing a tool to analyse the situation is complicated because each tool has strengths and weaknesses. Some tools are very expensive but go into fine details, whereas others are helpful for getting an initial picture to develop an outline of the gaps among identity, image, and reputation. To make a choice, it is helpful to ask the following questions: What is the matter of concern? What do I know already? What discretion do I have from my bosses? Which audience am I addressing? How much time do I have to analyse? How many resources do I have? Depending on the answers, it will be possible to choose the approach (i.e. inductive or deductive) and the right tool (i.e. quantitative and qualitative). Without any presumption of a single 'best way', we will next discuss a number of tools for different purposes. Table 2.2 provides an overall summary of when to measure what. The reader should take these as mere suggestions and general guidelines that can be reconsidered in each specific and real situation.

Assessing organisational culture

A number of subjective or objective tools can be used to assess organisational culture. The choice between them depends on available time, resources, and the discretion to make decisions. Cultural analysis involves 'discovering how insiders experience and construct their world' (Hatch 1997: 201). Thus, we should choose methods to avoid an exclusive observer's perspective. The ethnographic method permits the grasping of people's meanings and interpretations and the insider point of view; it mostly involves qualitative data (Gregory 1983). If one does not have sufficient resources for an ethnographic study, one might opt for a quantitative tool. The latter incurs the disadvantages of decontextualising the analysis, but gives a first broad-brush picture of the situation. Quantitative tools depend on a priori typologies that categorise cultural phenomena (Cameron and Ettington 1988). One might start with rituals and rites that define a culture (see Trice and Beyer 1984); catalogues of dimensions such as emotionality, personalisation, subordination, conservatism, isolationism, and antipathy (Bate 1984); power distance, uncertainty avoidance, individualism, and masculinity (Jaeger 1986; Hofstede 1980); speed and risk cultures (Deal and Kennedy 1983; see also chapter on risk communication); authoritarianism and participation (Sriramesh *et al.* 1996); paranoid, avoidant, charismatic, bureaucratic and politicised (Kets de Vries and Miller 1986); and hierarchical, market-oriented, adhocracy, and clan type (Cameron and Quinn 1999). To diagnose these cultural distinctions, standardised questionnaire-based instruments can be used.

Organisational identity: who are we?

To assess organisational identity, one might start with the official corporate communication and ask members whether they agree or disagree with these statements (van Riel and Carroll 2001; Illia *et al.* 2004). This approach identifies how closely corporate statements match the members' organisational identity, thereby directly identifying the (de)coupling of the 'organisational I-us' and the 'corporate me-us'. Framing the questions exclusively from corporate-level projections will not pick up those features that arise at the organisational level, but are not projected at the corporate level. To avoid this blind spot, one needs to choose an integrative approach and start with what organisational values and features are actually perceived (van Rekom *et al.* 2006; van Rekom 1998; Illia 2009a, 2009b). Mapping discourses, conversations, and the everyday use of language is useful (Cheney 1991; Boje 1991). Alternatively, researchers elicit people's thinking about the organisation by probing opinions or obtaining accounts of critical episodes (Flanagan 1954; Dutton and Dukerich 1991; Illia 2009a, 2009b, Illia and Balmer 2012). These approaches are mostly inductive and qualitative; sometimes they are a combination of qualitative and quantitative analysis. Their value lies first in identifying the collective identity by starting from members and their identities, then moving to an ad hoc assessment that is specific for the organisation at a specific time. If it is required to develop an assessment of the organisation over time, it is preferable to start with a predefined list of categories that can be easily implemented and assessed repeatedly in fixed or variable time intervals (Gioia and Thomas 1996).

Establishing a desired identity: who do we want to be?

A number of tools and procedures help with brainstorming and discussing the desired identity of the organisation (van Rekom and van Riel 2000). The Cobweb method by Bernstein (1984) and the Star method by Lux (1995) explore identities through a workshop with top managers. The Cobweb method is inductive and asks to come up with a list of features managers believe to be important for the organisation's future. The subsequent discussion lowers the number of features in the list to a consensus of which ones are best for their organisation. The Lux Star method is deductive and starts with a given list of potential attributes. These features are clustered, again by consensus, into key characteristics of typical companies' attitudes, needs, constitutions, heritage, and goal orientations. Both methods enable managers to brainstorm ideas using numbers and charts. However, these methods do not allow managers to come up with a corporate story or description. For this purpose, one might follow the procedure suggested by Collins and Porras (2000), who proposed a series of questions to help managers explore the core ideology, core purpose, and envisioned future of the organisation. Going beyond brainstorming, this helps managers construct and agree upon a vivid description of the organisation that can be circulated through corporate storytelling.

Corporate identity: how shall we project ourselves?

To assess the corporate identity statements as they are projected, in the context of reviewing them, managers can again rely on several approaches depending on purpose. If the purpose is to rebalance the degree by which the company projects itself either by emotional appeal or functional exposition, the methods of choice are content analysis of messages, images, videos, etc. (van Riel 1995; Cornelissen 2011; de Chernatony 2001). This will help managers identify how concrete attributes of a company and its products and services warrant an emotional message, expressing a specific personality or corporate key values. Alternatively, one might analyse the corporate story, its symbols, and language used. The corporate story is only sustainable if it presents a credible description based on which the company is able to engage with its stakeholders (van Riel 1995). A sensitive analysis of 'who we are' (see previous discussion) offers the basis upon which to create a story that gives a positive impression of the company.

On the other hand, physical objects can be chosen as symbols whose meanings carry connotations that cover the organisational context (van Riel 1995; van Riel and Fombrun 2007). In this approach, corporate graphical systems are analysed, including the name of the company or its products and services, logo and corporate slogan, typeface colour, and design of messages. For example, an analysis of a logo should allow us to judge whether the logo is consistent with the overall image and identity of the company (Olins and Selame 2000). It should assess what meanings it creates and how memorable it is (Henderson and Cote 1998).

A good logo, beyond being literally consistent with the organisational objectives, also has correct recognition (people are able to remember it), false recognitions (it reminds people of other things), and affective meaning (people have an emotional reaction to it) as well as being easily anchored (it evokes something already familiar in nature or culture). Finally, the analysis might include a wide range of corporate projections in advertising, promotions, press releases, and internal communications (van Riel 1995; Rossiter and Percy 2001). The latter analysis is best performed in situations where a repositioning is required as a result of radical changes.

Image and reputation: how are we perceived?

The literature identified four ways to assess image and reputation. First, one considers that audiences and stakeholders observe companies as corporate persona (Berens and van Riel 2004), attributing personality traits that 'account for consistent patterns of behaviours' (Pervin 1989: 4). Here the question is not attitude (i.e. good or bad qualities), but attributed traits arising from the perceiver and his/her experience and imagination of the organisation. Researchers have developed questionnaire tools to assess this persona-type image. The corporate personality scale (Davies *et al.* 2003) assumes that the company comes to life, using an analogy of an individual's personality. This leads to an important question: What type of personality might this be? Projective methods such as Photosort (van Riel 1995; van Riel and Fombrun 2007; van Riel *et al.* 1998) follow a similar line of analogical reasoning and assess the company through association with pictures of people and their expected personality (if company A is person X, what newspaper would they read; what car would he/she drive; where would he/she go on holiday; what is his/her gender type, etc.). This projective assessment is useful for engineering corporate repositioning.

In situations in which audiences experience potentially failed expectations, it is more useful to assess the image of people's attitudes towards the company (van Riel *et al.* 1998). The attitude is a balanced sum of ideations about an object, including beliefs, evaluations, and intentions (Fishbein and Ajzen 1975). Questionnaires are constructed using Likert scales (5-point scales; agree-disagree) or Osgood semantic differentials (Snider and Osgood 1969). The advantage of attitude scales is that they are easily constructed and replicated over time as well as for benchmarking the company against competitors. The weakness arises from the fact that the act of research can, at least to a certain extent, shape respondents' attitudes. Various favourability biases, such as social desirability and acquiescent response bias, can occur. To avoid biased results, one might opt to analyse the company's image according to what stakeholders expect from the company and how far they trust it. Several tools can be used to assess corporate credibility (Newell and Goldsmith 2001) as reliable, honest, and benevolent actions of the company (Berens and van Riel 2004) or simply as the reputation of companies (Fombrun *et al.* 2000). Whereas the former focus on what is relevant to the perceiver's direct experience with the organisation, the latter maps how people evaluate the company (as being good or bad) according to various sources and criteria – namely, its emotional appeal, product and services, financial performance, vision and leadership, workplace environment, and social responsibility. Finally, one can measure the image of a company on how audiences experience the company's specific comportment. Caldwell and Coshall (2002) developed this type of analysis with museums, analysing how visitors perceive museums based on how employees treat them and what atmosphere they experience at the museum.

Field identity: how is our field perceived? How are we projecting the collective at the inter-organisational level?

Assessing field identity involves assessing both (a) how the field (i.e. an industry or market niche) projects its image or reputation and (b) how the group of companies project themselves as a group, collectively. With regard to the first, managers can use the previously suggested tools for reputation and image assessment and apply them at the industry or market niche level. Meanwhile, for the second area, current studies suggest analysing the stories that corporations are projecting collectively to identify the main stories that companies in the same field share. An example of how to assess these stories is provided by Illia and Zamparini (2012). Another way to measure a field's identity from the perspective of how companies are projecting as a collective is to analyse the various categories to which companies refer. An example of this is provided by Rao *et al.* (2003, 2005).

The risks of dynamic adjustment: narcissism or neuroticism

Faced with several potential gaps, any managerial attempt to take dynamic control of the corporate persona runs two basic risks of over-adjustment: internal over-adjustment to the gap within (i.e. organisational narcissism) and external over-adjustment (i.e. corporate neuroticism) reacting to the difference between internal and external assessments of image and identity, or the internal–external gap (see Hatch and Schultz 2002). Developing a neurotic hyper-adaptation means, for example, that new image positioning is considered only from its external point of view (either audiences or field level); the gap is adjusted towards the audience's perceptions, forgetting the cultural heritage of the company itself. For example, in repositioning the corporation, one considers relevant only the gap between what managers desire the company to be and what external audiences' expectations are, without making allowances for how employees support the repositioning or if the company, in its current state, is really capable of moving in the new direction. A well-known example is the case of Lego (see Hatch and Schultz 2002; Ravasi and Schultz 2006), which has repositioned itself in the market of video games in the last decades. In its zeal to please consumers, the company projected a totally new corporate image and identity as a video game company. However, this repositioning did not work out, and the company ended in crisis. One possible explanation is that the company ignored its own cultural heritage of providing kids with another kind of amusement. Lego's culture was still that of making plastic bricks and developing kids' imaginations through creative building of physical objects, rather than virtual contests. By focusing purely on the external point of view, Lego reminded us that working on the external–internal gap ignores important gaps that might open between what is communicated and who the organisation really is. Woody Allen made a film, *Zelig*, illustrating this over-adjustment with the character of Zelig, who immediately accommodates to the characteristics of the interlocutor. If the interlocutor is overweight, Zelig becomes overweight; if the other is short in stature, Zelig shrinks; if the other stammers, Zelig stammers as well. In the end, it is not clear who Zelig really is despite the documentary features of the film.

By contrast, in a narcissist adjustment to a gap situation, the problem is considered only from an internal perspective, without considerations of external audiences and stakeholders. The gap is reduced by working from within the existing organisational culture and identity. An example is provided by the old company Royal Dutch Shell (see Hatch and Schultz 2002; Fombrun 1996; Greyser and Klein 1996; Zyglidopoulos 2002). In 1995, the company planned to dump the Brent Spar, a decommissioned oil rig, into the North Sea. It had taken advice from engineers who considered the dumping to the bottom of the sea as the most environmentally friendly option. It had also obtained the consent of the regulators – in this case, the British government – at the time. This decision followed the organisation's deeply rooted culture, according to which expert advice is the best and only advice to consider in these situations. However, external audiences, particularly environmental activists, considered this option to be not environmentally friendly, dismissing Shell's expert advice as biased. Royal Dutch Shell had analysed the situation without scoping out stakeholders' expectations and had to face implications for the company's reputation. Public protest, stirred by Greenpeace and other environmental organisations, resulted in a consumer boycott of its petrol stations across Europe and forced Shell to retract its plan and tow the platform to Norway for deconstruction of the installation on shore. What Shell had considered to be its strength and good image making – the dumping choice was the scientifically best option – did have contrary effects as Shell's scientific rationale conflicted with public opinion. Thus, to avoid the blindness of a purely within-culture internal perspective, as in the case of Royal Dutch Shell, it is important to also consider gaps between what the organisation projects and how it is perceived by outsiders. Following the good practice of past successes rooted in the organisational culture – in the case of Shell, a culture of sound science and engineering advice and regulatory consent – is not sufficient for controlling reputational risks arising from a variety of stakeholders. A similar reputation and field-/industry-level legitimacy disaster emerged for the international agrochemical corporation Monsanto, which in the mid 1990s unleashed genetically modified soybeans on European consumers. Monsanto was focused on its own culture of revolutionising food production with the new science of genetic engineering and had worked hard to get farmers on board. It did everything to secure the support of regulatory authorities in the US and in Europe. However, it did not consider the consumers and food retailers, who were not Monsanto's primary market, although they were the market of the farmers and retailers. The reluctance of consumers to adopt GM food exploded in Monsanto's face with a vengeance and led to a crisis of the entire 'genetic engineering revolution' at the turn of the millennium. The arising great GM food debate has had global repercussions (see Durant *et al.* 1998; Bauer and Gaskell 2002; Gaskell and Bauer 2006).

Conclusion: the need for empirical evaluation and analysis

At the corporate communication level, the analogy between individuals and corporate persona can be beneficial. However, what might be problematic for an individual seems normal for a collective – namely, maintaining multiple identities. The management of corporate persona has to deal with the complications arising from multiple stakeholders on the one hand and from differences in giving and giving off impressions, from organisational identity and corporate projections, and from ideal corporate image and perceived reality on the other. These parallel processes of internal and external perceptions, expressions, projections, and reflections run the risk of decoupling and developing gaps. Yet a sustainable corporate persona is built on some consistency of these parallel processes.

It is well known that the first casualty of any strategic action is the plan. The strategic control of a company's corporate persona is a risky endeavour; it can fail in many ways and must consider unintended consequences, which require reconsidering the plan. We highlighted the risks of over-adaptation in particular (i.e. corporate narcissism and corporate neuroticism). To avoid these risks of exclusively internal or external orientation, corporate communication managers need to develop empirical evaluations and constantly monitor the situation. To this end, a range of methods and tools have been presented in this chapter which allow tracking both internal and external perceptions of the organisation. It thus appears that successful corporate persona management involves strategic interventions in conjunction with empirical evaluation of its intended outcomes as well as its unintended consequences.

Note

1 The authors thank Martin W. Bauer for his insights into and comments on the chapter.

References

Albert, S. and Whetten, D. A. (1985) 'Organisational identity', in Cummings, L. L. and Staw, B. M. (eds) *Research in Organisational Behavior*. Greenwich, CT: JAI Press, 263–95.
Alversson, M. (1990) 'Organisation: From Substance to Image?', *Organisation Studies* 11(3): 373 94.
Arthur W. Page Society (2007) *The Authentic Enterprise*, New York City.
Arthur W. Page Society (2012) *Building Belief: A New Model for Activating Corporate Character and Authentic Advocacy*, New York City.

Balmer, J. M. T. (2012) 'Corporate brand management imperatives: custodianship credibility and calibration', *California Management Review* 54: 3–28.

Balmer, J. M. T. and Greyser, S. A. (2002) 'The multiple identities of the corporation', *California Management Review* 44(3): 72.

—— (2003) *Revealing the Corporation: Perspectives on Identity, Reputation, Corporate Branding and Corporate-Level Marketing*, London: Routledge.

—— (2006) 'Corporate marketing: integrating corporate identity, corporate branding, corporate communications, corporate image and corporate reputation', *European Journal of Marketing*, 40(7–8): 730–41.

Balmer, J. M. T., Stuart, H. and Greyser, S. A. (2009) 'Aligning identity and strategy: corporate branding at British Airways in the late 20th century', *California Management Review* 51(3): 6– 23.

Bate, P. (1984) 'The impact of organisational culture on approaches to organisational problem-solving', *Organisation Studies* 5: 43–66.

Bauer, M. W. and Gaskell, E. (eds) (2002) *Biotechnology – the making of a global controversy*, Cambridge: CUP.

Berens, G. and van Riel, C. B. M. (2004) 'Corporate associations in the academic literature: Three main streams of thought in the reputation measurement literature', *Corporate Reputation Review* 7(2): 161–78.

Bernstein, D. (1984) *Company Image and Reality: A critique of corporate communications*, Eastbourne: Holt, Rinehart and Winston.

Boje, D. M. (1991) 'The storytelling organisation: A study of story performance', *Administrative Science Quarterly* 36(1): 106–26.

Caldwell, N. and Coshall, J. (2002) 'Measuring brand associations for museums and galleries using repertory grid analysis', *Management Decision* 40(4): 383–92.

Cameron, K. S. and Ettington, D. R. (1988) *The Conceptual Foundations of Organisational Culture. Higher Education: Handbook of Theory and Research*, New York: Agathon.

Cameron, K. S. and Quinn, R. E. (1999) *Diagnosing and Changing Organisational Culture*, Reading, MA: Addison-Wesley.

Cheney, G. (1991) *Rhetoric in an organisational society: Managing multiple identities*, Columbia, SC: University of South Carolina Press.

Christensen, L. A. and Askegaard, S. (2001) 'Corporate identity and corporate image revisited', *European Journal of Marketing* 35: 292–315.

Collins, J. C. and Porras, J. I. (2000) *Built to Last: Successful habits of Visionary Companies*, London: Random House.

Cooley, C. H. (1902/56) *Human Nature and Social Order*, New York: Scribner's.

Cornelissen, J. (2011) *Corporate communication: a guide to theory and practice*, London: Sage.

Davies, G., Chun, R., Da Silva, R. and Roper, S. (2003) *Corporate Reputation and Competitiveness*, London: Routledge.

Deal, T. E. and Kennedy, A. A. (1983) 'Culture: a new look through old lenses', *Journal of Applied Behavior Science* 19(4): 498–505.

de Chernatony, L. (2001) *From brand vision to brand evaluation*, Oxford: Butterworth Heinemann.

DiMaggio, P. J. and Powell, W. (1983) 'The iron cage revisited: institutional isomorphism and the collective rationality in organisational fields', *American Sociological Review* 48: 147–60.

Dowling, G. R. (1986) 'Managing your corporate images', *Industrial Marketing Management* 15: 109–15.

Durant, J., Bauer, M. W. and Gaskell, G. (eds) (1998) *Biotechnology in the public sphere: a European source book*, London: Science Museum Publications.

Dutton, J. E. and Dukerich, J. M. (1991) 'Keeping an eye on the mirror: Image and identity in organisational adaptation', *Academy of Management Journal* 34(3): 517–54.

Dutton, J. E., Dukerich, J. M. and Hartquail, C. V. (1994) 'Organisational images and member identification', *Administrative Science Quarterly* 39: 243–8.

Erickson, E. H. (1980) *Identity and the life cycle*, New York: Newton.

Etang, J. (2008) *Public relations: concepts practice and critique*, Los Angeles: Sage.

Fiol, C. M. and Romanelli, E. (2011) 'Before identity: The emergence of new organisational forms', in Solomon, G.T. (ed.) *Organisation Science*, Articles in Advance: 1–15.

Fishbein, M. and Ajzen, I. (1975) *Belief, Attitude, Intention, and Behavior: An Introduction to Theory and Research*, Reading, MA: Addison-Wesley.

Flanagan, J. C. (1954) 'The critical incident technique', *Psychological Bulletin* 51: 327–58.

Fombrun, C. (1996) *Reputation. Realizing Value from the Corporate Image*, Boston: Harvard Business School Press.

Fombrun, C. J. and Shanley, M. (1990) 'What's in a name? Reputation building and corporate strategy', *Academy of Management Journal* 33(2): 233–58.

Fombrun, C. J., Gardberg, N. A. and Sever, J. M. (2000) 'The reputation quotient: A multi stakeholder measure of corporate reputation', *The Journal of Brand Management* 7(4): 241–55.

Gaskell, G. and Bauer, M. W. (eds) (2006) *Genomic and Society. Legal, Ethical and Social Dimensions*, London: Earthscan.

Gioia, D. A. (1998) 'From individual to organisational identity', in Whetten, D. A. and Godfrey, P. C. (eds) *Identity in organisations: Building theory through conversations*, Thousand Oaks, CA: Sage, 17–32.

Gioia, D. A. and Chittipeddi, K. (1991) 'Sensemaking and sensegiving in strategic change initiation', *Strategic Management Journal* 12(6): 433–48.

Gioia, D. A. and Thomas, J. B. (1996) 'Identity, image, and issue interpretation: Sense making during strategic change in academia', *Administrative Science Quarterly* 41: 370–403.

Gioia, D. A., Schultz, M. and Corley, K. G. (2000) 'Organisational identity, image and adaptive instability', *Academy of Management Review* 25(1): 63–81.

Glynn, M. A. (2008) 'Beyond constraints. How institutions enable identities', in Greenwood, R., Oliver, C., Suddaby, R. and Sablin-Andersson, K. (eds) *The Sage handbook of organizational institutionalism*, 413–30, Thousand Oaks: Sage.

Goffman, E. (1959) *The presentation of self in everyday life*, New York: Doubleday Anchor Books.

Greenwood, R. and Suddaby, R. (2006) 'Institutional entrepreneurship in mature fields: The big five accounting firms', *Academy of Management Journal* 49: 27–48.

Gregory, K. L. (1983) 'Native-view paradigms: Multiple cultures and culture conflicts in organisations', *Administrative Science Quarterly* 28(3): 359–76.

Greyser, S. A. (2009) 'Corporate brand reputation and brand crisis management', *Management Decision* 47(4): 590–602.

Greyser, S. A. and Klein, N. (1996) 'The Brent Spar Incident: A Shell of a Mess', Harvard Bussiness School Case Study, 597–013.

Hatch, M. J. (1997) *Organisation theory: Modern Symbolic and Postmodern Perspectives*, New York: Oxford University Press.

Hatch, M. J. and Schultz, M. (2002) 'The dynamics of organisational identity', *Human Relations* 55(8): 989–1018.

—— (2008) *Taking the brand initiative*, San Francisco: Jossey-Bass.

Henderson, P. W. and Cote, J. A. (1998) 'Guidelines for selecting or modifying logos', *Journal of Marketing* 62(2): 14–30.

Hilton, C. (2012) 'Hilton's Chris Brooks on engaging the media via Twitter', *PR News*, online, available at: http://www.prnewsonline.com/mediarelations/PR-News-Q-and-A-Hiltons-Chris-Brooks-On-Engaging-the-Media-Via-Twitter_17216.html, 18 October 2012 (accessed on subscription, November 2012).

Hofstede, G. (1980) *Culture's Consequences: International Differences in Work-Related Values*, Beverly Hills, CA: Sage Publications.

Illia, L. (2003) 'Passage to cyberactivism: how dynamics of activism change', *Journal of Public Affairs* 3: 326–37.

—— (2009a) *Changing Organisational Identity: Understanding Difficulty to Change and Members' Concerns*, Saarbruche: Dr Müller VDM Verlag.

—— (2009b) 'Exploring how to diagnose members' concerns to change what is core in organisations', *Journal of Applied Behavioral Science* 45(4): 550–80.

Illia, L. and Balmer J. M. T. (2012) 'Corporate communication and corporate marketing: Their nature, histories, differences and similarities', *Corporate Communications: An International Journal* 17(4): 415–33.

Illia, L. and Bauer, M. (2009) *Corporate Communication as Reputation Management*, unpublished manuscript prepared for the course of corporate communication, London School of Economics and Political Science.

Illia, L. and Zamparini, A. (2012) *Building a Corporate Image through Identity Stories: An Empirical Investigation*, paper presented at the Reputation Conference 2012, Milan, unpublished manuscript.

Illia, L., Schmid, E., Fishbach, I., Hantgartner, R. and Rivola, R. (2004) 'An issues management perspective to corporate identity: The case of a governmental agency', *Corporate Reputation Review* 7(1): 10–24.

Jaeger, A. M. (1986) 'Organisation development and national culture: where's the fit?', *Academy of Management Review* 11: 178–90.

Jenkins, R. (1996) *Social identity*, London: Routledge.

Kets de Vries, M. F. R. and Miller, D. (1986) 'Personality, culture, and organisation', *Academy of Management Review* 11: 266–79.

Kotler, N. and Kotler, Ph. (1998) *Museum Strategy and Marketing: Designing Missions, Building Audiences, Generating Revenue and Resources*, San Francisco: Jossey Bass Wiley.

Lammers, J. C. (2011) 'How institutions communicate: Institutional messages, institutional logics, and organisational communication', *Management Communication Quarterly* 25: 154–82.

Lerpold, L., Ravasi, D., van Rekom, J. and Soenen, G. (eds) (2007) *Organisational Identity in Practice*, London: Routledge Publishing.

Lounsbury, M. and Glynn, M. A. (2001) 'Cultural entrepreneurship: stories, legitimacy, and the acquisition of resources', *Strategic Management Journal* 22: 545–64, doi: 10.1002/smj.188.

Lux, P. G. C. (1986) 'Zur Durchführung von Corporate Identity Programmen', in Birkigt, K. and Stadler, M. (1986) *Corporate Identity, Grundlagen, Funktionen und Beispielen*, Landsberg an Lech:Verlag, Moderne Industrie.

Lux, P. G. C. (1995) 'Durchführung von Corporate Identity Programmen', in Birkigt, K., Stadler, M. M. and Funck, R. (1995) *Corporate Identity, Grundlagen, Funktionen, Fallbeispiele*, 8th edn, Landsberg/Lech: Verlag Moderne Industrie, 593–614.

Mead, G. H. (1934) *Mind, Self and Society*, Chicago: University of Chicago Press.

Newell, S. J. and Goldsmith, R. E. (2001) 'The development of a scale to measure perceived corporate credibility', *Journal of Business Research* 52(3): 237–8.

Olins, W. (1989) *Corporate Identity: Making Business Strategy Visible through Design*, London: Thames and Hudson.

Olins, W. (2008) *The Brand Handbook*, London: Thames & Hudson Ltd.

Olins, W. and Selame, E. (2000) *Corporate Identity Audit. A company self assessment tool*, London: Prentice Hall.

Pervin, L. A. (1989) *Personality, Theory and Research*, New York: John Wiley.

Price, K., Gioia, D. A. and Corley, K. (2008) 'Reconciling scattered images: Managing disparate organisational expressions and impressions', *Journal of Management Inquiry* 17(3): 173–85.

Rao, H., Monin, P., Durand, R. (2003) 'Institutional change in Toque Ville: Nouvelle cuisine as an identity movement in French gastronomy', *American Journal of Sociology* 108(4): 795–843.

—— (2005) 'Border crossing: Bricolage and the erosion of categorical boundaries in French gastronomy', *American Sociological Review* 70(6): 968–91.

Ravasi, D. and Schultz, M. (2006) 'Responding to organisational identity threats: Exploring the role of organisational culture', *Academy of Management Journal* 49(3): 433–58.

Rosenfeld, P., Giacalone, G. A. and Riordan, C. A. (2002) *Impression management: building and enhancing reputations at work*, London: Thomson Learning.

Rossiter, J. R. and Percy, L. (1987) *Advertising and Promotion Management*, New York: McGraw-Hill.

Rossiter, J. R. and Percy, L. (2001) 'The a-b-e model of benefit focus in advertising', in Reynolds, T. J. and Olson, J. C. (eds) *Understanding Consumer Decision Making*, Mahway, NJ: Lawrence Erlbaum Associates, 183–214.

Schein, E. H. (1980) *Organizational Psychology*, 3rd edn, Englewood Cliffs, NJ: Prentice-Hall.

Schein, E. H. (1984) 'Coming to a new awareness of organisational culture', *Sloan Management Review* 25(2): 3–16.

Schenkler, B. R. (1985) *The self and the social life*. New York: McGraw-Hill.

Shannon, C. E. and Weaver, W. (1949) *The Mathematical Theory of Communication*, Urbana, IL: University of Illinois Press.

Smidts, A., Pruyn, A. T. H. and van Riel, C. B. M. (2001) 'The impact of employee communication and perceived external prestige on organisational identification', *Academy of Management Journal* 49(5): 1051–62.

Smircich, L. (1983) 'Concepts of culture and organisational analysis', *Administrative Science Quarterly* 28(39): 339–58.

Snider, J. G. and Osgood, C. E. (1969) *Semantic Differential Technique: A Sourcebook*, Chicago: Aldine.

Soenen, G. and Moingeon, B. (2002) 'The five facets of collective identities', in Moingeon, B. and Soenen, G. (eds) *Corporate and Organisational Identities*, London: Routledge, 13–34.

Sriramesh, K., Grunig, J. E. and Dozier, D. M. (1996) 'Observation and measurement of two dimensions of organisational culture and their relationship to public relations', *Journal of Public Relations Research* 8(4): 229–61.

Tedeschi, J. T. (1981) *Impression management theory and social psychological research*, New York: Academic Press.

Trice, H. M. and Beyer, J. M. (1984) 'Studying organisational culture through rites and ceremonials', *Academy of Management Review* 9: 653–69.

van Rekom, J. (1998) *Corporate identity: Development of the concept and a measurement instrument*, unpublished doctoral dissertation, Erasmus University, Rotterdam, the Netherlands.

van Rekom, J. and van Riel, C. B. M. (2000) 'Operational measures of organisational identity: A review of existing methods', *Corporate Reputation Review* 3(4): 334–50.

van Rekom, J., van Riel, C. B. M. and Wierenga, B. (2006) 'A methodology for assessing organisational core values', *Journal of Management Studies* 43(2): 175–201.

van Riel, C. B. M. (1995) *Principles of Corporate Communications*, Harlow: Prentice Hall.

—— (2012) *The Alignment Factor: Leveraging the Power of Total Stakeholder Support*, London: Routledge.

van Riel, C. B. M. and Balmer, J. M. T. (1997) 'Corporate identity: the concept, its measurement and management', *European Journal of Marketing* 31(5–6): 340–55.

van Riel, C. B. M. and Carroll, C. E. (2001) *We who are many from one body: the impact of multiple identities on organisational identification*, paper presented at the special organisational identity workshop, Amsterdam, 15 December 2001.

van Riel, C. B. M. and Fombrun, C. (2007) *Essentials of Corporate Communication*, London: Routledge.

van Riel, C. B. M., Stroeker, N. E. and Maathuis, O. J. M. (1998) 'Measuring corporate images', *Corporate Reputation Review* 1(4): 313–26.

Whetten, D. (2006) 'Albert and Whetten revisited: Strengthening the concept of organisational identity', *Journal of Management Inquiry* 15(3): 219–34.

Wry, T., Lounsbury, M. and Glynn, M. A. (2011) 'Legitimizing nascent collective identities: Coordinating cultural entrepreneurship', *Organisation Science* 22: 449–63.

Zyglidopoulos, S. C. (2002) 'The social and environmental responsibilities of multinationals: Evidence from the Brent Spar case', *Journal of Business Ethics* 36(1–2): 141–51.

3   Managing the brand from within

Almudena González del Valle Brena

Introduction

This chapter tries to tap into the relationship between corporate branding and internal communications. It should highlight the importance of internal communication and employees for managing organisations nowadays, and the importance of internal communication in supporting a corporate brand. Employees play a valuable role in the delivery and strengthening of corporate brands, and most specifically in service brands (Papasolomou and Vrontis 2006).

In times of organisational change, managing the corporate brand from within becomes important. Organisational change may refer to an organisation-wide change rather than to small changes; i.e. a change of mission, restructuring operations, the adoption of major technologies or mergers (French *et al.* 2009). When change happens in a changing business and socio-economic environment, the issue turns out to be crucial.

Scholars have recognised the value of internal communication and relationships in change management implementation, helping companies to achieve success (Barrett 2002). Schultz *et al.* (2000:1) propose that the interests (Human Resources, communications, marketing, strategy, and accounting) which promote ideas such as organisational identity, branding and reputation within business are in great need of supporting one another. However, many companies do prefer to keep these interests separated, favouring a low-key profile as communicators. This dynamic also affects how the brand is perceived by the internal stakeholders, as well as external. Sharma and Kamalanabhan (2012) in their study of internal corporate communication and its impact on internal branding, note that human resources and internal corporate communication functions should be integrated in order to disseminate corporate brand information effectively. Perhaps there is more than one brand that needs to be managed and monitored and communicated and, in the end, strategy must serve all stakeholders, and this means that the whole company must work together to achieve effective performance (Schultz *et al.* 2000).

The need to create and manage the corporate brand from within the company arises when companies want to offer stakeholders its benefits. In this chapter the case of a multinational testing, inspection and certification services company will be depicted, focusing on its local subsidiary in Spain. In the past years, this subsidiary has undergone mergers and faced difficult business times. A new communications strategy is to be implemented to encourage employees to enliven the corporate brand and to actually help corporate branding. This chapter is not a research piece, but a description of a communications and corporate branding issue from an internal point of view.

Corporate branding and organisational, internal communications

Corporate branding emphasises that the organisation itself, rather than the products created and marketed by the corporation, represents the main point of differentiation and competitive advantage in the marketplace (Schultz 2005). According to Hulber (2006) the reason for increased interest in corporate branding can be broadly explained by three main factors: differentiation, transparency and cost reduction. Corporate branding goes beyond product branding in that the corporate brand is based on the corporate identity, that is, the organisation's values, its promises, and its attitudes towards stakeholders and the environment. Nevertheless, corporate branding loses much of its intentionality unless managers realise that stakeholders have different world views and opinions of organisations. These diverse stakeholders' attitudes must be identified if corporate brand management is to be successful (Hulber 2006). Balmer and Gray (2003) write that a corporate brand's values are latent in the values of the organisation's founders, owners, management and personnel. A prerequisite for successful branding is, among others, proactively managing stakeholders' relations.

According to Balmer (1995) there are no universal rules when managing corporate brands. Papasolomou and Vrontis (2006), for example, studied integrated marketing approaches in the UK retail bank industry. Their research showed that the integrated marketing perspective had the potential to integrate all staff in the branding process and create an organisational culture that set the foundation for building a strong corporate brand. Melewar *et al.* (2012) in their study of corporate branding agenda and avenues for future research write that understanding how individuals (e.g. employees, managers, customers and other stakeholders) experience, interpret and influence the corporate brands is, therefore, critical in managing corporate brands. They posit several possible research questions on the topic, such as how to uncover how individuals experience or interpret the influence of corporate brands, or what it is that motivates employees to enliven the brand. Answering these questions may require exploring organisational factors and practices that may trigger brand identification (ibid.). De Chernatony and Dall'Olmo Riley (1999) propose that the success of service brands depends on carefully nurtured relationships between the employees and customers, which develop staff's and consumers' respect for certain functional and emotional values of the brand. Corporate branding necessitates a different management approach. It requires greater emphasis on factors internal to the organisation, paying greater attention to the role of employees in the brand building process (Harris and de Chernatony 2001).

Faust and Bethge (2003) stated that, in corporate branding, too much attention is spent in the development and implementation of external messages and promotional actions at the consumer touch points, but no emphasis is put on the internal customers, the employees. By applying brand design principles to internal communications, large organisations can accelerate the process of changing employee attitudes and employee behaviour. Stuart and Rodríguez-Cánovas (2013) in Chapter 7 of the present book state that corporate brands formerly emphasised two main stakeholders: the customers and shareholders. However, employees are now being recognised for the crucial role they play in enacting the corporate brand. Employees are already stakeholders and receive corporate brand messages. The stronger employees' identification, commitment and loyalty to the brand, the more successful the (re)branding strategy will be as the more probable it is that managers and employees will act in accordance with the corporate brand values (Harris and de Chernatony 2001). In corporate rebranding processes, for instance, one major pitfall is that employees often receive information after the strategy is initiated (Gotsi and Andriopoulos 2007). Internal branding influences employees' brand identification, brand commitment and brand loyalty (Punjaisri and Wilson 2007).

Employees need time to adjust to organisational changes, especially when the change involves a certain degree of organisational personnel downsizing because of a merger or acquisition (Marris 1986). Not much attention has been paid in research to brand integration in company mergers. In this respect, Balmer and Dinnie (1999) proposed the merger mix, comprising stakeholders' finance, corporate identity and corporate communications, to overcome the narrow focus on financial issues. In fact, a thorough literature analysis on mergers and acquisitions and brand management may be found in Brexendorf and Kernstock's Chapter 5 in this book.

Organisational communication includes all communication aimed at increasing the reputation of and satisfaction with the organisation (Elving *et al.* 2012). Internal communication is considered as all communication within the organisation with the objective of informing organisational members on what their tasks are and what changes in tasks are at hand (Elving 2005). Most branding communication is directed externally, but it is often the internal stakeholders who define the brand and provide the actualisation of the experience (Vasudevan 2008). Effective internal communication is crucial for successful organisations as it affects the ability of strategic managers to engage employees and achieve objectives. Management plays a key role in the development and maintenance of corporate identity, including paying particular attention to the internal aspects of the process.

Communication may help an organisation achieve its goals. Communication management becomes a strategic management activity when it helps in securing the long-term functioning of the organisation in society, as opposed to being an operational activity, just implementing top management decisions (Elving *et al.* 2012). Effective internal communication is crucial for successful organisations as it helps strategic managers to achieve objectives by engaging employees (Welch and Jackson 2007). Since internal communication takes place within dynamic environments, 'effective internal corporate communication should enable understanding of the relationship between ongoing changes in the environment and the consequent requirement to review strategic direction' (ibid.: 190).

The chapter goes on with the study of a low profile in communications activities efforts to leverage on a strong and historical corporate brand, managed from within the organisation using internal communications. In trying to implement an ambitious strategic plan for future growth, the company must overcome dispersion in the corporate brand after acquisition processes in Spain. Managing the brand from within the company presents the challenge of purposeful internal communications.

BV: a trusted brand

Bureau Veritas is a world leader in testing, inspection and certification services,with 2011 revenue of €3.4 billion (Bureau Veritas 2012) and approximately 59,000 employees around the world. Bureau Veritas offers innovative solutions that go beyond simple compliance with regulations and standards, reducing risk, improving performance and promoting sustainable development. Bureau Veritas core values include integrity and ethics, impartial counsel and validation, customer focus and safety at work. Bureau Veritas is recognised and accredited by major national and international organisations. On their corporate website, among other strong assets, Bureau Veritas cites the 'brand and reputation', because they hold a strong brand built over 180 years.

History

Founded in Antwerp in 1828, in what is today Belgium, the Information Office for Maritime Insurance had a simple mission: to give shipping underwriters up-to-date information on premiums in use at commercial centres and provide precise information on the state of ships and equipment.

In 1829, the company was renamed Bureau Veritas, adopted the emblem of Truth as its official logo and published its first Register of some 10,000 ships. In 1833 the head office transferred from Antwerp to Paris, where a branch office had been set up in 1830.

On 24 October 2007, Bureau Veritas became listed on the Paris Stock Exchange. In the past few years, Bureau Veritas has streamlined its organisation to enable a better market focus and keep a strong growth momentum. The Group is now structured along eight global businesses: marine, industry, inspection and in-service verification, construction, certification, commodities, consumer products and government services and international trade, and is present in 140 countries. Strong organic growth and more than 100 acquisitions in the past 20 years have pushed BV into a leadership position on our market.

The 2012–15 strategic plan is very solid, based on an in-depth analysis of Bureau Veritas's markets and service portfolio and a detailed review of growth opportunities. Beyond financial goals, the plan provides the road map around which to mobilise teams in order to unleash the full potential of the company.

> My role is to achieve this vision by motivating and inspiring the Group's management teams. All Bureau Veritas managers are dedicated to the plan's execution and I will personally support their efforts, including by interacting with public authorities and large clients. The Group is on track to reach its 2015 objectives and to keep growing beyond.
>
> (Didier Michaud-Daniel, CEO, 2011 Activity Report)

Bureau Veritas focuses its corporate social responsibility efforts on areas where it can have the greatest impact and where the need for action is most pressing, such as protecting employee health and safety, ensuring business integrity, preserving the environment and supporting key stakeholder relationships. While growing significantly and integrating numerous acquisitions over the past five years, the company also has achieved significant progress in its CSR priority areas. This continuing commitment will be a key element in implementing the BV 2015 strategy.

Moving forward with confidence

The company's strategic plan for 2015 targets a strong growth, aiming at becoming an international services group with global revenue of around 5 billion euros and 80,000 employees by the end of 2015: 'The targets of the strategic plan are to be delivered through three main levers: the Group's human resources policy, its excellence in IT/IS tools and its continuously adapting organisation' (BV press release, September 2011).

Marc Boissonet, Senior Vice President Communication and Marketing, in an online interview in 2009 acknowledged that Bureau Veritas communicates externally to its clients mostly about regulations and certification, testing or inspection issues. Nothing was said about internal stakeholders, though. In the strategic plan outlined in September 2011, the Group stated its intention to leverage on internal pillars, such as to promote the 'One company' dimension.

The strategic plan adjective for Spain is 'revitalising', along three main lines: adapt to market demand, leverage the number one position and revitalise the company (BV Strategic Plan presentation, September 2011).

Looking into the certification services unit, Bureau Veritas Certification Spain's total 2011 sales amounted to 21 million euros in systems certification, and two million euros in product certification services. These figures position BVC as second market leader right after main competitor AENOR, a standardisation body which also leads the product certification market in Spain. BVC Spain is divided into six regions, employing a total of 130 employees in the certification tasks, such as schedulers, auditors, sales and management. Certification resources are segmented in seven units: supply chain unit; sustainability; agro-food; product and customised, large contracts; operations, performance, IT and back office; technical area; and sales. As of October 2012 their product portfolio involved 49 per cent non-QHSE (quality, health and safety, and environmental) activities. Certification also holds an e-learning and in-classroom training unit.

Bureau Veritas in Spain concentrates 16 brands; some of them are corporate brand names and commercial brands at the same time. In 2007, Bureau Veritas acquired ECA Certificación, a Spanish certification. From 2008 onwards, several brands belonging to ECA Global were modified, in an effort to ease the identification with Bureau Veritas. However, in this reshaping of the brands, some ECA logos were maintained, although incorporating a reference to Bureau Veritas. The divisions ECA Certification and ECA Training did adopt Bureau Veritas as brand, and their logos and corporate image were changed to those of Bureau Veritas. Nevertheless, as of December 2012, colours, logos and website were still different.

Following a period of downsizing, due to both an economic environment in crisis in Spain, and the merger process itself, ECA employees amount to some 3,000. The challenge in communication and corporate branding terms is to recoup the brand and its use across all BV Spain units. The strategic lines are drawn to reinforce trust and feelings of belonging among employees. Within Spain, the old ECA name is still widely recognised in some country regions – such as Catalonia – more than in others.

Internal communications is under the direct command of Human Resources. Under the newly appointed Senior VP for Communication and Marketing position, this function should undergo some foreseeable structuring. Still, there have been some internal efforts towards achieving 'One company', such as promoting and communicating an employee perks and promotion plan, '*BVeneficiate*', or the salary compensation plan 'BV Plus'. These two plans are communicated to all employees, across the Spanish subsidiary, regardless of their 'origins' – i.e. ECA or Bureau Veritas. According to BV Spain directors, the challenge that the company faces right now is to actually create and communicate the integration of brands, and to implement the 'one brand' environment stated in the general strategic company plan for the years to come.

Conclusion

Crises are defining moments for a company, but they are the right moments for employee engagement. The strategic role of communication in change processes and changing environments is well documented in scholarly literature. This case study aims at exploring the relationship between internal communications and corporate branding in a company where communications has always been geared towards external stakeholders, and in subtle and counselling ways. Leveraging on a strong, historical, trusted corporate brand, internal communications shows potential to help in achieving strategic objectives for future years. Integrating internal communications within a strategic function would develop a long-term internal branding effort.

Although this case illustrates a potential road ahead, the issue and the future results may be of interest to other managers within the industrial, testing or certification sector, as well as companies integrating brands and resources after an acquisition. Therefore, proper research needs to be carried out in the field of managing brands from an internal communication perspective.

References

Anixter, J. (2003) 'Transparency or not: Brand Inside: Brand Outside ™: The most obvious yet overlooked next source for the brand's authentic evolution', in Ind, N. (ed.) *Beyond Branding*, London: Kogan Page.

Balmer, J. M. T. (1995) 'Corporate branding and connoisseurship', *Journal of General Management* 21(1): 24–46.

Balmer, J. M. T. and Dinnie, K. (1999) 'Merger madness: The final coup de grâce', *Journal of General Management* 24(4): 53–70.

Balmer, J. M. T. and Gray, E. R. (2003) 'Corporate brands: What are they? What of them?', *European Journal of Marketing* 37(7–8): 972–97.

Barrett, D. J. (2002) 'Change communication: using strategic employee communication to facilitate major change', *Corporate Communications: An International Journal* 7(4): 219–31.

Barrow, S. and Mosley, R. (2005) *The Employer Brand®. Bringing the Best of Brand Management to People at Work*, UK: John Wiley & Sons, Inc.

Berthon, P., Ewing, M. and Hah, L. L. (2005) 'Captivating company: dimensions of attractiveness in employer branding', *International Journal of Advertising* 24(2): 151–72.

Boissonnet, Marc (2009) interview, online, available at: http://www.dailymotion.com/video/xafyma_culture-com-web-agency-webo-webo-fr_news#.UMjxBoNFyHM (accessed 12 December 2012).

Brexendorf, T. O. and Kernstock, J. (2013) 'Corporate brand integration in mergers and acquisitions', in Balmer, J. M. T., Illia, L. and González del Valle Brena, A. (eds) *Contemporary Perspectives on Corporate Marketing*, London: Routledge.

Brønn, P. S. (2002) 'Corporate communication and the corporate brand', in Brønn, P. S. and Wiig, R. (eds) *Corporate Communication: A Strategic Approach to Building Reputation*, Oslo: Gyldendal Akademisk, 91–106.

Bureau Veritas (2012) websites, available at: http://www.bureauveritas.com; http://www.bureauveritas.es (accessed November 2012).

Cheney, G. and Christensen, L. (2001) 'Organisational identity: linkages between internal and external communication', in Jablin, F. M. and Putnam, L. L. (eds) *The New Handbook of Organisational Communication*, Thousand Oaks, CA: Sage, 231–70.

Chong, M. (2007) 'The role of internal communication and training in infusing corporate values and delivering brand promise: Singapore Airline'' Experience', *Corporate Reputation Review* 10(3): 201–12.

Davies, G. and Chun, R. (2002) 'Gaps between the internal and external perceptions of the corporate brand', *Corporate Reputation Review* 5(2–3): 144–58.

de Chernatony, L. (2001) *From Brand Vision to Brand Evaluation*, Oxford: Butterworth Heinemann.

de Chernatony, L. and Dall'Olmo Riley, F. (1999) 'Experts' views about defining services brands and the principles of services branding', *Journal of Business Research* 46(2): 181–92.

Doorley, J. and García, H. F. (2007) *Reputation management, the key to successful public relations and corporate communications*, London: Routledge.

Elving, W. J. L. (2005) 'The role of communication in organisational change', *Corporate Communications: An International Journal* 10(2): 129–38.

Elving, W. J. L., van Ruler, B., Goodman, M. and Genest, Ch. (2012) 'Communication management in the Netherlands: Trends, developments, and benchmark with US study', *Journal of Communication Management* 16(2): 112–32.

Faust, B. and Bethge, B. (2003) 'Looking inward: How internal branding and communications affect cultural change', *Design Management Journal* 14(3): 56–63.

French, R., Rayner, Ch., Rees, G., Rumbles, S., Schermerhorn, J. Jr, Hunt, J. and Osborn, R. (2009) *Organisational Behaviour*, UK: John Wiley & Sons Ltd.

Gotsi, M. and Andriopoulos, C. (2007) 'Understanding the pitfalls in the corporate rebranding process', *Corporate Communications: An International Journal* 12(4): 341–55.

Harris, F. and de Chernatony, L. (2001) 'Corporate branding and corporate brand performance', *European Journal of Marketing* 35(3–4): 441–56.

Hatch, M. J. and Schultz, M. (2001) 'Are the strategic stars aligned for your corporate brand?', *Harvard Business Review* 79(2): 128–34.

—— (2003) 'Bringing the corporation into corporate branding', *European Journal of Marketing* 37(7–8): 1041–64.

Hulber, J. (2006) 'Integrating corporate branding and sociological paradigms: A literature study', *Journal of Brand Management* 14: 60–63.

Ind, N. (1997) *The Corporate Brand*, London: Macmillan Business.

—— (2004) *Living the brand*, 2nd edn, London: Kogan Page.

King, C. (2008) 'Internal branding: Exploring the employee's perspective', *Journal of Brand Management* 15(5): 358–72.

Knox, S. (2004) 'Positioning and branding your organisation', *Journal of Product & Brand Management* 13(2): 105–15.

Marris, P. (1986) *Loss and change*, London: Routledge & Kegan Paul.

Melewar, T. C., Gotsi, M. and Andriopoulos, C. (2012) 'Shaping the research agenda for corporate branding: avenues for future research', *European Journal of Marketing* 46(5): 600–608.

Mitchell, C. (2002) 'Selling the brand inside', *Harvard Business Review* 80(1): 99–105.

Papasolomou, I. and Vrontis, D. (2006) 'Building corporate branding through internal marketing: the case of the UK retail bank industry', *Journal of Product & Brand Management* 15(1): 37–47.

Podnar, K., Golob, R. and Jancic, Z. (2011) 'Identification with an organisation as a dual construct', *European Journal of Marketing* 45(9–10): 1399–1415.

Punjaisri, K. and Wilson, A. (2007) 'The role of internal branding in the delivery of employee brand promise', *Journal of Brand Management* 15: 57–70.

Punjaisri, K. and Wilson, A. (2011) 'Internal branding process: key mechanisms, outcomes and moderating factors', *European Journal of Marketing* 45(9–10): 1521–37.

Schultz, M. (2005) 'A cross-disciplinary perspective on corporate branding', in Schultz, M., Antorini, Y. M. and Fabian, F. C. (eds) *Corporate Branding: Purpose, People, and Processes*, Copenhagen: Copenhagen Business School Press, 23–56.

Schultz, M., Hatch, M. J. and Larsen, M. H. (2000) *The expressive organisation: linking identity, reputation, and the corporate brand*, New York: Oxford University Press.

Sharma, N. and Kamalanabhan, T. J. (2012) 'Internal corporate communication and its impact on internal branding: Perception of Indian public sector employees', *Corporate Communications: An International Journal* 17(3): 300–322.

Stuart, H. and Rodríguez Cánovas, B. (2013) 'Corporate branding: an employee perspective', in Balmer, J. M. T., Illia, L. and González del Valle Brena, A. (eds) *Contemporary Perspectives on Corporate Marketing*, London: Routledge.

van Riel, C. B. (1995) *Principles of Corporate Communication*, London: Prentice-Hall.

Vasudevan, S. (2008) 'The role of internal stakeholders in destination branding: Observations from Kerala Tourism', *Place Branding and Public Diplomacy* 4(4): 331–5.

Welch, M. and Jackson, P. R. (2007) 'Rethinking internal communication: a stakeholder approach', *Corporate Communications: An International Journal* 12(2): 177–98.

Part 1

Managing corporate brands

Integrating them with multiple and national identities

4 Confucius meets Mao

The changing Chinese national identity and implications for nation branding

Ying Fan

Introduction

On 14 January 2011 a gigantic bronze sculpture of Confucius was unveiled with great ceremony in front of the National Museum of China on Tiananmen Square, Beijing, the political heart of China, where Chairman Mao's portrait has been dominant since the People's Republic of China (PRC) was inaugurated in 1949. Confucius is the first non-revolutionary figure to be honoured in such a highly symbolic place. Traditional Chinese culture encompasses diverse and sometimes competing schools of thought, including Confucianism, Taoism, Buddhism, and a host of regional cultures. Nevertheless, Confucianism is undisputedly the most influential thought, which forms the foundation of the Chinese cultural tradition and still provides the basis for the norms of Chinese interpersonal behaviour (Pye 1972). In the history of mankind, no one else has experienced a more dramatic comeback in recent years than Confucius. For the greater part of two thousand years, Confucius (551–79 BC), or Master Kong as he is called in Chinese (孔夫子), had been used by emperors as an indispensable tool to maintain their feudalistic rule. However, for most of the twentieth century, Confucianism had been reviled, denounced and abandoned first by radical intellectuals in the 1920s and later by communists for 40 years. Mao regarded the ancient philosopher as the Number One Enemy of the Chinese nation and publicly condemned Confucius to history's dustbin. The renaissance of Confucianism came with economic reform in the 1980s when traditional values were brought back as a solution to the increasing social problems.

The appearance of Confucius's statue on Tiananmen Square has been seen as a symbolic political statement that China has, at last, re-found Confucius and embraced the traditional culture. Surprisingly, the co-inhabitancy of Confucius and Mao lasted less than 100 days. On 22 April 2011, the statue mysteriously disappeared for no apparent reason. A National Museum spokesman said he did not know what had happened, and city officials would not comment. Some sources said it had been moved inside the museum. There was much speculation that the Leftists in the Chinese Communist Party (CCP) opposed the presence of the statue on the square. The reconciliation between Confucius and Mao turned out to be premature and short-lived.

This chapter studies recent changes in the Chinese national identity and national symbols. It examines the differences between political identity and cultural identity, and the differences between official national symbols and popular national icons. The implications for nation branding are also discussed.

China has changed

Profound changes have taken place in China since the CCP decided to adopt the reform and open door policy in December 1978. In the past 34 years, China's economy has achieved an average annual growth of 8.5 per cent, reversing previous economic decline that put the country on the verge of bankruptcy, and transforming the country into the world's second largest economy. China is widely predicted to overtake the United States to become the world's largest economy by 2020.

The Chinese are obsessed with anything that has a symbolic value, especially rankings and numbers. A case in point is the Beijing Olympic Games. The opening ceremony proper began on 8 August 2008 with a contemporary drum sequence performed by 2,008 Fou drummers. The LED-embedded Fou drums and their glowing drumsticks were lit up by the drummers. In formation, the drummers lit their drums to form giant digits (in both Arabic and Chinese numerals) to count down the final seconds to the Games and herald the start of the opening time of 8:08 p.m. local time on 8 August 2008 (08:08-08/08/08), as the number eight is considered lucky in Chinese culture. This most impressively coordinated extravaganza was filled with colour, symbolic and historical references. A common feature in Chinese media coverage includes: the world's largest exporter, the highest number of skyscrapers, the fastest trains, the longest bridge, the best Olympic Games ever held, the biggest holder of US government debt – the list is very long. On reading these facts, one could easily forget that China is still a poor developing country with a per capita GDP at 7,600 US dollars (at purchasing power parity), 126th in the world (CIA 2011). While China is reported to have more than a million millionaires in 2011, it is an appalling fact that tens of millions of people still live on under one US dollar per day.

With a history going back five thousand years and a population of 1.3 billion people, China is far from a monolith. There are many Chinas – it is a nation full of contrasts, contradictions and paradox. The biggest paradox is the fact that the world's most populous capitalist country is still ruled by the same Communist Party that has been in power for 63 years. In the aftermath of changes in Eastern Europe in 1989, many experts in the West predicted the demise of the CCP and the imminent collapse of China. These experts were proved to be utterly wrong. The reasons are multiple and complex but some are obvious. China is different from the USSR, and the CCP has changed with the times. Trying to keep a foot in both camps, the CCP managed to cling to a vestige of communist ideology while embracing capitalism wholeheartedly. Founded in 1921, the CCP is the world's second largest organisation after the Catholic Church with 80 million members – the same as the population of Germany. One should not underestimate the adaptability of China in general, and the CCP in particular. With a large pool of top-notch talents, the CCP holds the ability to control many aspects of Chinese society – even to changing the weather, as was demonstrated during the Beijing Olympics. As no other viable political force could emerge in the foreseeable future, the prospect is that the CCP will continue to reform and transform itself gradually in the years to come.

National identity

Social identity theory (Tajfel 1974) stipulates that people categorise their social group memberships (e.g. their race/ethnicity, their nation) and identify with the groups that they belong to. The cultural history of humanity is a successive differentiation of processes of identification (Smith1992: 58). National identity, as the product of such process, refers to a sense of shared continuity, shared memories of history and the collective belief in a common destiny (Smith 1992: 58). Here shared does not mean that it is felt or interpreted in the same way (Geisler 2005), as each individual will have different feelings or intensity of feeling about it.

National identity can be studied at different levels: collective identity and individual identity, as people will have different feelings or different strengths of feeling about it. A nation has multiple identities. It is important to distinguish political identity from cultural identity. Political identity, or state identity, is the official identity imposed by the ruling elite on the nation, for example, through a compulsory curriculum in education systems (Ho and Law 2003). Political identity may or may not be accepted by citizens of the country, is transient and more easily subject to change. On the other hand, cultural identity is the collective identity that is widely accepted by the people, more enduring, and passed on from one generation to another. National identity, in essence, is the cultural identity of a nation's people.

To understand the transformation in China and its global implications, one cannot ignore the central role of identity in shaping the nation's domestic developments and foreign relations (Callahan 2009). National identity is also the product of domestic and international politics. China's national development strategy has two pillars: creating a harmonious society domestically and pursuing peaceful development internationally, which is based on the idealised view of Chinese civilisation being open to the world, and tolerant of outsiders. The reality is a different picture. With growing inequality and rampant corruption, social unrest has increased dramatically. The country is grappling with more acute social problems than ever before, according to a report from the Chinese Academy of Social Sciences (BBC 2009).

Having undertaken a great range of transformations over the last three decades, China is now well on the way to becoming the next superpower. However, China has suffered a serious identity crisis for a long time as the nation needs to find something to fill the vacuum left by the discredited communist ideology.

China's national identity

For many centuries in the history of mankind, China was a prominent world power with the largest economy that at its peak in the 1830s accounted for more than 30 per cent of the world total GDP. The first Opium War with Britain (1839–42) marked the beginning of the so-called Century of National Humiliation (百年国耻1839–49). This humiliation ended when the CCP 'liberated' the country and founded the socialist New China (PRC) in 1949. The major events in modern Chinese history are highlighted in Table 4.1. Meissner (2006) provides an excellent account of China's long search for national identity from the middle of the nineteenth century to the modern time that is divided into five distinctive periods. Starting in 1978 with the initiation of the economic reform and open-door policy, the last period is still ongoing and characterised by a number of developments: the rejection of orthodox communist ideology, the renaissance of Confucianism, and the invasion of Western thoughts such as individualism and consumerism.

The bygone Century of National Humiliation still casts its shadow over China and this victim mentality is a key element in the contemporary Chinese national identity. It is particularly handy for the CCP for two reasons. First, all Chinese problems, old or new, could be attributed to the oppression and exploitation that China suffered under the imperial powers. Second, saving China from the ruin of

Table 4.1 Milestones in China's modern history

Year	Major event
1839	The First Opium War
1860	Yuanming Yuan (Imperial Palace) burnt down by French and British troops
1911	The overthrow of the Qing dynasty, the founding of the Republic of China
1921	The founding of the CCP
1937–45	The war against Japanese occupation
1949	The CCP victory, the founding of the People's Republic of China
1958–61	Great Leap Forward (Great Famine)
1966	Start of the Cultural Revolution
1976	Mao's death, the end of the Cultural Revolution
1978	The CCP announced the economic reform
1989	Crackdown on protests in Tiananmen Square
2001	China joined WTO
2008	Beijing Olympics
2010	China became the world's second largest economy

Source: Compiled by the author

'semi-colonial and semi-feudalist' status legitimates the CCP's right to govern. Ironically, China's identity was relatively simple in Mao's era. For Mao's China (1949–76), Mao, as the 'right' symbol for the nation, characterised perfectly what China stood for at the time: revolutionary, radical, proletarian, Red China and Third World. While the Chinese state has played an instrumental role in promoting patriotism, its success in constructing a pessoptimist identity for the nation is said to have derived from the interactive and intersubjective nature of China's identity construction (Callahan 2009). Ordinary citizens in China are closely involved in the production and consumption of Chinese nationalism, and concepts such as 'civilisation and barbarism' and 'national pride' are prevalent in popular discourse (Li 2010).

A yin-yang perspective

Yin-yang is a part of ancient Chinese philosophy that describes how polar opposites or seemingly contrary forces are interconnected and interdependent in the natural world, and how they give rise to each other in turn. Underlying all the yin-yang thinking is the fundamental aim of creating a truly inclusive system of thought – a system that would embrace and explain the phenomena of the entire universe (Fung 1983: 131). Yin-yang philosophy, which has received some affirmation from both modern physics and analytical psychology, maintains that there are two overall forces, the masculine and the feminine, inherent in all phenomena and responsible, by their interactions, for the emergence and dissolution of all things. Yin and Yang describe a world in which people and things, structures, and processes, make up different expressions of a continuum, rather than irreconcilable opposite (Lessem 1998: 94).

Yin-yang is a system of dialectical duality thinking (Li 1998: 416). The yin-yang tenet is so powerful and pervasive that no aspect of Chinese civilisation – whether philosophies, beliefs, science, medicine, literature, politics, arts – has escaped its imprint. In simple terms, the doctrine teaches that all things and events are products of two elements, forces, or principles: yin, which is negative, passive, weak, and destructive; and yang, which is positive, active, strong, and constructive. The theory is associated with that of the Five Elements (Metal, Wood, Water, Fire and Earth) which may be taken as an elaboration of the yin-yang idea but actually adds the important concept of rotation, i.e. the things succeed one another as the Five Elements take their turns (Fung 1983: 19; Chan 1963: 244; Chok 2006: 412).

Yin and yang are complementary opposites that only exist in relation to each other and interact within a greater whole, as part of a dynamic system. Everything has both yin and yang aspects, but either of these aspects may manifest more strongly in particular objects, and may ebb or flow over time. The continuous interplay between these primal bipolar forces of yin and yang, the positive and the negative, creates stress, change, and harmony in the universe as humans know it (Osgood and Richards 1973: 380). When yin reaches its extreme, it becomes yang; when yang reaches its extreme, it becomes yin. The pure yin is hidden in yang, and the pure yang is hidden in yin (Ji *et al.* 2001: 450).

The best way to understand China – the nation and its complex identities – is from a yin-yang perspective. A number of seemingly opposite factors are inter-twined and interact with each other in the construction of national identity, which emerges through the interplay of both positive and negative feelings in a dynamic that intertwines China's domestic and international politics and turned China into a 'pessoptimist nation' (Callahan 2009).

The Chinese civilisation is widely regarded as the longest continuous surviving civilisation dating from ancient times, despite the fact that China had been conquered by northern nomads as well as other foreign invaders such as Mongols and Manchus. What is uniquely amazing about the Chinese civilisation is that, instead of imposing its own culture on China, the invaders had been assimi-lated into Chinese culture and become a part of it. It is interesting to note that China's self-perception follows a typical yin-yang pattern, oscillating between high pride and low self-esteem. After profound changes over the last three decades, China is facing the dilemma of repositioning itself. For example, is China still a poor developing country or a developed one? During a period of fundamental changes national identity in China can never be defined as a simple construct but a complex mixture that contains both a sense of cultural superiority and low self-esteem; victim mentality and Great Power mind-set; traditional values and Western ideas.

Identity crisis

China has been said to suffer from an identity crisis for such a long time that a question should be asked first: what is actually in crisis? On the surface, there is indeed a serious crisis in the state political identity – defined by the CCP in 1979 – a socialist country based on the Four Cardinal Principles (Socialist Path, People's Democratic Dictatorship, Leadership of the CCP, and Marxist–Leninist–Mao Zedong Thought). Though unchanged on paper, this identity has been almost completely broken by the fundamental changes in Chinese society over the last three decades so that only one principle, the leadership of the CCP, still stands. On the other hand, it would be inaccurate to claim that China's cultural identity is in a big crisis. Since the late nineteenth century, Chinese culture has become a convenient scapegoat for all the country's problems, ranging from feudal oppression to economic backwardness. Radical reformers from different generations conclude that in order to modernise, China must replace its tradi-tional culture with a wholesale Westernisation. Ironically, this was also echoed by the 2010 Nobel Prize winner Liu Xiaobo who insists that China needs to have 300 years of colonisation because Chinese culture is inferior to Western culture. Liu's politically motivated view is absurd and totally indefensible. A nation's culture needs to be critically reviewed and renewed from time to time, but its core values cannot be discarded as that is what makes that nation unique in the world. Chinese culture, as represented by Confucianism and other ancient schools, has dominated Chinese political and social life for more than two thousand years. Its influence has seen ups and downs, but its core values have never been in a 'crisis'.

Even during the darkest time of the Cultural Revolution, such cultural identity was simply hidden or dormant, but never entirely erased. Chairman Mao, an ardent communist himself, was deeply influenced by the traditional cultural values; and his thinking – Mao Zedong Thoughts or Maoism – bears heavy marks of Chinese culture. The CCP, the very organisation that Mao created and developed to rule China, is in fact the successor to the bureaucratic system that the First Emperor (259–210 BC) of the Qin Dynasty invented.

People talk about crisis as they fear change. Changes in the reality have caused problems on two sides. Internally, people have become confused and started to question their identity. On the international stage, China's external image has become seriously outdated, if not totally distorted. The identity crisis in China refers to a number of different issues: first, the growing gaps between the state-sanctioned political identity and the rapidly changing reality; second, the gap between political identity and cultural identity. People are caught between the political identity and cultural identity, and confusions deepen about questions such as who we are and what we want to be. Third, with the absence of a national religious faith, China needs to find a value system to fill the void left by the bankrupted communist ideology. It is in this context that the CCP rediscovered the value of Confucius and Confucianism: the core message in his teaching of deference to authority and the maintenance of societal harmony perfectly suits the Party's vision of a harmonious society.

National symbols

National symbols are conceptual representations of a nation that condense the knowledge, values, history and memories associated with the nation and increase people's sense of psychological identification with their nation (Firth 1973; Feshbach and Sakano 1997; Butz 2009). The first time a flag was used as an emblem of power may have been in China in 1122 BC when a white flag is said to have been carried before the founder of the Chow dynasty (Encyclopædia Britannica Online). National symbols are of paramount importance in understanding the fundamental mechanisms in forming national consciousness as well as in maintaining a national identity. Symbols such as flags, emblems, anthems, costume, special foods, and sacred objects express the sense of difference and distinctiveness of a community. Each of these elements articulates a vital dimension of the culture-community (Smith 1995: 131).

National symbols can be classified in different ways. Official national symbols include flags, anthems, and emblems. They may also include national dress, national colour, gemstone and floral emblems as shown in the Australian Government website (Australia Government 2012). A nation is a daily plebiscite, invented, imagined and ethno-symbolic community (Anderson 1991) which talks to itself through symbols, being a part of a mass media system that reveals a window into the historical fault lines within a given society (Geisler 2005). Some of the most common symbols of China are shown in Table 4.2, and this is by no means a complete listing.

Table 4.2 China's national symbols and icons

Official	National emblem National flag – Five-star Red Flag National anthem –'The March of Volunteers' Tiananmen Square Chairman Mao (in Tiananmen Square, and on RMB)
Historical	Confucius Yan and Huang Emperors The Great Wall Chinese characters Dragon Yellow River Four great inventions (compass, gunpowder, papermaking and printing)
Contemporary	Confucius Chinese language/characters Dragon The Great Wall Chinese cuisine Kung fu (Bruce Lee) Giant panda Celebrities (e.g. Yao Ming, an NBA player) Iconic buildings (e.g. Bird's Nest Stadium)
Humiliation	Yuanming Yuan Hong Kong (before returning to Chinese rule in 1997) 'Sick man of East Asia' 18 September 1931 (the day the Japanese occupied Manchuria) Nanking Massacre (300,000 civilians were murdered by Japanese troops in 1937)

Source: Compiled by the author

To differentiate from official national symbols, icon is the term used here to describe those individuals or objects that are regarded as a 'symbol' or representative of the nation at a specific time and event. They are widely recognised but, unlike official national symbols, are not necessarily endorsed by the State. For example, the Great Wall and Giant Panda are recognised Chinese icons worldwide but neither is officially acknowledged. Fashion is a significant expression of cultural identity (Tomlinson 2003). During the Cultural Revolution (1966–76), China was dubbed a nation dressed in dark grey Mao suits, which were widely worn among the entire male population as a symbol of proletarian conformity. The dress code in China has since become more diversified and more colourful, with the Western-style business suit being recognised as a popular symbol of modernity and success. There has been a recent surge in the wearing of traditional dress such as *qipao* (旗袍), which people choose in order to express a form of Chineseness.

Different groups will have different degrees of emotional attachment to these symbols or icons and interpret them differently. It is even possible that within individuals the associations with symbols can be rather ambivalent, with some situations and contexts producing positive, egalitarian associations, while other contexts evoke negative, aggressive associations with the same symbol. Particular types of associations may be activated and become influential in different contexts and situations (Butz 2009).

The meaning of a national symbol may be changed dramatically over time. For centuries, the Great Wall was a terrible reminder of the tyranny of the First Emperor of China (Qin Shihuang) when one million forced labourers died building the wall. A turning point came in 1935 with the theme song of a patriotic film, *the March of Volunteers*, which transformed the Great Wall from an evil national symbol into a positive one ('Let our flesh and blood forge our new Great Wall!'). The song was later adopted as the National Anthem of PRC in 1949. Apart from being one of the greatest mega engineering projects in the world, the Great Wall now symbolises the unified China and its glorious past.

The dragon (龙/龍) is another national symbol in China which has different meanings. Historically, the dragon symbolises potent and auspicious powers (especially relating to emperors or the imperial household). Chinese people regard themselves as the descendants of the dragon. The dragon is also a symbol of power, strength, and good luck when used in daily language: an outstanding and successful person is referred to as being a dragon (望子成龙 – *Hoping one's son to become a dragon*). Dragon is also a popular male name as Bruce Lee and Jackie Chan both used it. The Chinese dragon differs from the European dragon in both imagery and meaning; it has no wings and does not blow fire. There is a suggestion that the Chinese pinyin version 'Long' should be used in English to differentiate the Chinese dragon from the European dragon that is generally perceived as an evil symbol.

What are unique in China are the National Humiliation Symbols that play a crucial role in constructing a pessoptimist identity for the nation. A case in point is Yuanming Yuan (圆明园) – *the Imperial Garden of Perfect Brilliance* – which was looted and burned down by the invading British and French troops during the Second Opium War in1860. Yuanming Yuan has since become an icon of national humiliation; a testament to both Chinese civilisation and foreign barbarism (Callahan 2009: 16). The site of the ruins is a constant reminder of what China suffered under the oppression of Western imperial powers, and the lesson learned that a backward country was bound to be bullied (落后就要挨打).

Notably missing from the list of national symbols are Chinese brands. A strong brand can be a powerful symbol for the nation (Fan 2008a). The Japanese prime minister is quoted as saying that Sony and Matsushita (Panasonic) are the left and right faces of Japan. The image of the USA is largely shaped by omnipresent US-based global brands such as Coca-Cola and Nike. Despite being the world's largest exporter, with products sold to every corner of the world, China has a long way to go to create a number of global brands that not only help change the negative perceptions of the 'Made in China' label but also contribute positively to the nation's image.

Characters of national symbols

National symbols and cultural icons, like religious symbols, are often multi-referential and context based because different individuals or groups associate the same symbol with strikingly different concepts, memories, values, or emotions (Butz 2009: 796; Brown and MacGinty 2003). Hong Kong, ceded to Britain after the First Opium War, was for many years a national symbol of humiliation. Following the return of its sovereignty to China in 1997, it has become a positive national symbol of a successful global metropolis – a role model for other cities in China.

It is worthy of note that some symbols, such as the Great Wall, are for both internal and external use, while others are either for internal use only – for example, humiliation symbols such as Yuanming Yuan; or for external use only – for instance, the giant panda. While some symbols can be both historical and contemporary (Chinese characters), others are transient and temporary (a celebrity). National symbols are agents of social changes (Butz 2009); at the same time, social changes also produce new symbols or give a new meaning to old ones. Official symbols, though important for state political functions, have a rather limited impact on the general public: only a few people can accurately tell the meaning of their own national flag or emblem, let alone those of other countries. In contrast, it is the unofficial, popular icons that matter most in representing a nation's image on the world stage. Consider the impact of Disney on the image of the USA.

In 2006, a professor from Beijing University predicted that Chinese culture would have a real future only when Zhang Ziyi (an actress in 2000 movie *Crouching Tiger, Hidden Dragon*) was given as much importance as Confucius. He was also quoted as saying: 'A Yao Ming (an NBA player), or a Zhang Ziyi, is more effective than 10,000 copies of Confucian works'. His remarks triggered a heated debate on who best represents China (http://www.china.org.cn 2006). Thousands of Internet users who read the article online reacted furiously by arguing that Ms Zhang is no comparison for Great Master Confucius. While Ms Zhang's popularity may last another ten years, Confucius is for ever. However, the professor was perhaps misunderstood by his critics. China needs both historical symbols such as Confucius and contemporary cultural icons like Zhang. As representatives of popular Chinese culture, the latter are familiar to many foreigners and have been accepted as symbols of China. Pop icons and celebrities can be used as ambassadors or carriers for the promotion of Chinese culture.

In addition to the four categories listed in Table 4.2, there is a special type of icon in China: dissidents such as the imprisoned Nobel Prize winner Liu Xiaobo and artist Ai Weiwei. They are special because they are not 'Made in China' but products fabricated in the West for the purpose of humiliating China. Little known inside China, and with mediocre academic or artistic talent, these people are the darlings of Western media and governments. They are not China's conscience as portrayed in the West, but rather a tool used by the latter in Cold War-style propaganda to blacken China's image.

Symbols, identity and others

The advancement in information technology and the Internet have reduced the once expensive and time-consuming task of searching for information to a few clicks in seconds. However, huge gaps and barriers still exist in understanding between countries and cultures. A big barrier is information ethnocentrism. Most people in most countries know little and care less about countries other than their immediate neighbours; and even then their feelings are often a mixture of prejudice and ignorance (Olins 2002). In many cases, people have little knowledge even about their own country. A recent survey in the US showed that 26 per cent of the youth had no idea from which country America had achieved its independence. Among the countries mentioned were France, China, Japan, Mexico, and Spain (Marist Poll 2011). People can only develop an interest in, let alone affection for, another country on the basis of something they are familiar with. A simple and positive image in the form of a national icon would be invaluable in generating such interest.

Another barrier is the Self-Reference Criterion (SRC) – the unconscious reference to one's own cultural values or one's home country's frame of reference (Lee 1966). Culture is subjective. People in different cultures often have different ideas about other countries. It is virtually impossible for a person to observe foreign cultures without making references, perhaps unconsciously, back to his own cultural values (Onkvisit and Shaw 2008: 186). Through the tinted glasses of our own culture, we see things in a foreign culture not as they are, but as what we think they are or what we are (ibid.). This is because our perception is conditioned or framed by our own cultural values and experience.

National identity is shaped not only by a nation's people, but also by the environment surrounding them. Among the environmental influences, there are 'significant others', a term coined by Triandafyllidou (1998: 599) to refer to other nations that have significant influence. A nation's identity at a specific time is influenced by its world view, especially by how it sees other nations. This perception and knowledge of others provides the nation a context or reference point in defining its own identity (Fan 2008b). When it comes to impressions of foreign lands, people rely on the images constructed in the mass media to form an opinion (Wanta *et al.* 2004). Public opinion of foreign cultures is also heavily influenced by the media that play a critical role in shaping a nation's image in the minds of an international audience.

Coverage of China in the Western media is largely characterised by bigotry, stereotype and Cold War rhetoric. Western governments and media are so used to taking the moral high ground and lecturing China on human rights, freedom of speech and the rule of law that reports on China are often full of negative stories while turning a blind eye to its achievements. Several major media were recently exposed as having used fake photos in their reports of the so-called Jasmine Revolution in China (McGregor 2011). In comparison, coverage of the West in China, including in the official controlled media, is full of xenophilia. This might not be regarded as a total contradiction in a country that at the same time shows

Table 4.3 How China ranks and is ranked by other countries

(Out of 50)	China ranks	China ranked by
Australia	9	31
Brazil	21	33
France	16	43
Germany	1	31
India	44	21
Italy	17	44
Japan	48	50
Russia	24	23
UK	7	28
USA	6	35

Source: Compiled from Nation Brand Index

strong nationalism, if it is seen from a yin-yang angle. It has resulted in a kind of opinion trade deficit and its effect is shown in Table 4.3, where it can be seen that Chinese people ranked Western countries highly but their goodwill was not reciprocated. For example, China ranked Germany number 1 out of 50 countries while it was ranked by Germany 31 out of 50.

This comparison is critical to the study of national identity, as national identity and national image are relative constructs in which other nations play an important part (Fan 2008b). To be more precise, the self-image of a nation is influenced by how a nation sees other nations and is seen by other nations. The quest for defining the uniqueness of national identity is inseparable from the conception of others. National identity becomes meaningful only through contrast and comparison with other nations (Gellner 1964: 167–71; Kedourie 1992: 44–55; Trandafyllidou 1998: 596–9).

National symbols and nation branding

Nation branding has drawn growing interest from academics, policy makers and practitioners in recent years. Nation branding is essentially about managing a nation's image on the international stage (Fan 2010, 2006); it incorporates, absorbs, and embraces a wide variety of activities to form and project a loose and multifaceted yet coherent, interlocking, mutually supportive whole (Olins 2001a).

Identity and image are studied extensively in the context of business organisation. It is rather odd that national identity, national image and national symbols are seriously under-researched in the nation branding literature despite the utmost importance of such research in a time when nations are engaged in permanent and fierce competition with each other, for tourism, for inward investment, for exports and for political and cultural influence (Olins 2001b; Fan 2008c). A favourable image would give a nation a competitive advantage in the global marketplace. When the reality of a nation changes, the image has to change with it. It's bad for the national psyche when its reality is misunderstood, when changes in reality are not matched by changes in perception (Olins 1999). There is very little scholarly work that looks into the relationship between national identity and national symbols. Much remains unknown about how national symbols are created or selected, by whom and by what criteria (Tang *et al.* 2009), and how such symbols have evolved and changed in meaning and, most importantly, how the use of national symbols affects a nation's image internationally.

In the marketing literature, corporate image should be aligned with corporate identity (Davies and Chun 2002). Should a nation's image be aligned with its identity as well, reflecting changes? Although many organisations are much larger than some small nations, even a small nation is inherently far more complicated than a large organisation. Given the complexity in national identity construct, which aspect of national identity should be considered for the alignment? In reality, the perception of a nation is influenced by a variety of factors. National identity may or may not have anything to do with a nation's image abroad. In other words, national identity and national symbol/image are not that closely related as in the organisational context. For example, the Joan Miró sun symbol is recognised internationally as representing Spain but, strictly speaking, it is not a national symbol but merely a tourism logo, with no strong link to the Spanish national identity.

Study of national symbols and their links to national identity is a promising new direction for research in nation branding as it would help answer the important questions of who or what best represents a nation to the target international audience, and how a nation communicates its 'new' identity to the outside world. Yin-yang thinking offers a new perspective that helps better understanding of the complex and paradoxical constructs of national identity and national symbols.

Conclusion

In the contest on Tiananmen Square in 2011, it seems that Mao won and Confucius lost. However, it is a rather different picture if one looks beyond this short episode at broad context. The rehabilitation of Confucianism is all but completed. The Great Master is now worshipped in hundreds of Confucius temples around the country; TV programmes popularising his teaching have attracted millions; books promoting Confucian values are best-sellers. More significantly, Confucius's sayings are embedded into people's daily communications and still guide their thinking and behaviour just as they have done for more than two thousand years. Internationally, Confucius is a new great nation brand for China, helping promote China's soft power with the opening of over 320 Confucius Institutes in many countries. Confucius has been adopted as a Father Christmas-like symbol of avuncular Chineseness (*The Economist* 2011a). Confucius's place in Chinese history and culture has been re-established.

In contrast, Mao remains a controversial figure and his place in history is yet to be assessed (*The Economist* 2011b). The official line is that Mao is 70 per cent good and 30 per cent bad. Is Mao a national hero who was the father of the New China that ended the Century of National Humiliation; or a historical villain who was responsible for millions of unnatural deaths during the Great Leap Forward (in other words Great Famine, 1959–62) and the Cultural Revolution (1966–76)? There is no single or simple answer to the question as much depends on which political side one takes. Despite his prominent position on Tiananmen Square and on the Chinese currency, the RMB, Mao now generally has a low profile in the official media. Until major changes take place in China's political systems that end the CCP's monopoly of power, Mao is still indispensable to the CCP and there is little prospect of an objective assessment.

Confucius and Mao are both dead, but as potent national symbols they are really alive and continue to exert immense opposing influences on modern-day politics and social life in China, via symbolic communication over the long term between the dead and the living (Armstrong 1982: 8). During this communication, Confucius and Mao will be relentlessly re-imaged and reinterpreted to suit contemporary needs. What is extraordinary is how wide open is the struggle to associate either of them with such different national projects. The array of possibilities is as broad and diverse as the multistranded Chinese political spectrum (Friedman 1995: 292). Mao dominated China in the twentieth century, but he is undoubtedly a transient figure in the book of Chinese history. The day will come when Confucius comes back to Tiananmen Square after the departure of Mao.

Questions for discussion

- Is it possible to draw a clear distinction between political identity and cultural identity?
- If national identity cannot be defined as a simple construct, should a nation's image be aligned with its national identity? And, if yes, which aspect of national identity should be considered by the alignment?
- A nation's identity is shaped by its people and its external environment. To what extent do you think that your national identity is influenced by so-called significant others?
- Social and cultural changes in a country affect the currency of symbols and icons that its people identify with. Take a closer look at your favourite national symbol. Why do you think it is important? Has its meaning changed over the years? Is it the best way to represent your country in a nation branding campaign?
- What is the relationship between national identity, national symbols and a nation's image? According to the yin-yang tenet, opposite factors interact with each other in the construction of national identity. Is national image also formed in the same fashion?

References

Anderson, B. (1991) *Imagined communities: reflections on the origin and spread of nationalism*, London: Verso.

Armstrong, J. (1982) *Nations Before Nationalism*, Chapel Hill: University of North Carolina Press.

Australia Government (2012) online, available at: http://australia.gov.au/about-australia/our-country/our-national-symbols (accessed 26 March 2012).

BBC (2009) 'Social unrest "on the rise" in China', online, available at: http://news.bbc.co.uk/1/hi/8425119.stm (accessed 4 December 2012).

Bechhofer, F. and McCrone, D. (2009) 'National identity, nationalism and constitutional change', in Bechhofer, F. and McCrone, D. (eds) *National Identity, Nationalism and Constitutional Change*, UK: Palgrave Macmillan, online, available at: http://www.palgrave.com/PDFs/9780230551343.pdf (accessed 4 December 2012).

Brown, K. and MacGinty, R. (2003) 'Public attitudes toward partisan and neutral symbols in post-Agreement Northern Ireland', *Identities: Global Studies in Culture and Power* 10: 83–108.

Butz, D. A. (2009) 'National symbols as agents of psychological and social change', *Political Psychology* 30(5): 779–804.

Callahan, W. A. (2009) *China: the Pessoptimist Nation*, UK: Oxford University Press.

Chan, W. A. (1963) *A Source Book in Chinese philosophy*, US: Princeton University Press.

China Daily (2011) online, available at: http://europe.chinadaily.com.cn/china/2011-01/04/content_11802239.htm (accessed 26 March 2012).

China.org.cn (2006) online, available at: http://www.china.org.cn/english/2006/May/168519.htm (accessed 26 March 2012).

Chok, M. C. (2006) *Chinese Leadership Wisdom from the Book of Change*, Hong Kong: Chinese University Press.

CIA (2011) *The World Factbook*, online, available at: https://www.cia.gov/library/publications/the-world-factbook/geos/ch.html (accessed 26 March 2012).

Davies, G. and Chun, R. (2002) 'Gaps between the internal and external perceptions of the corporate brand', *Corporate Reputation Review* 5(2–3): 144–58.

Economist, The (2011a) 'Rectification of statues: Confucius as soft power, but the message gets confused at home', online, available at: http://www.economist.com/node/17969895 (accessed 26 March 2012).

Encyclopædia Britannica online, available at: http://search.eb.com/eb/article-9034458 (accessed 4 December 2012).

—— (2011b) 'China's online debate: Mao versus Mao', online, available at: http://www.economist.com/blogs/banyan/2011/06/chinas-online-debate (accessed 20 March 2012).

Fan, Y. (2006) 'Nation branding: what is being branded?', *Journal of Vacation Marketing* 12(1): 5–14.

—— (2008a) 'Country of origin, branding strategy and internationalisation: the case of Chinese piano companies', *Journal of Chinese Economic and Business Studies* 6(3): 303–19.

—— (2008b) 'Self-perception and significant others: A conceptual framework for nation image', paper presented at the Sixth Conference of Asia Academy of Management, Taipei, 14–16 December.

—— (2008c) 'Soft power: the power of attraction or confusion', *Place Branding and Public Diplomacy* 4(2): 147–58.

—— (2010) 'Branding the nation: towards a better understanding', *Place Branding and Public Diplomacy* 6(2): 97–103.

Feshbach, S. and Sakano, N. (1997) 'The structure and correlates of attitudes toward one's nation in samples of United States and Japanese college students: a comparative study', in Bar-Tal, D. and Staub, E. (eds) *Patriotism: In the lives of individuals and nations*, Chicago: Nelson-Hall, 91–108.

Firth, R. (1973) *Symbols: Public and private*, Ithaca, NY: Cornell University Press.

Friedman, E. (1995) *National Identity and Democratic Prospects in Socialist China*, New York: M. E. Sharpe.

Fung, Y. L. (1983/1934) *A History of Chinese Philosophy*, Vol. 11, New York: Princeton University Press.

Geisler, M. E. (2005) (ed.) *National Symbols, Fractured Identities: Contesting the National Narrative*, Lebanon, NH03766: Middlebury College Press.

Gellner, E. (1964) *Thought and Change*, London: Weidenfeld & Nicholson.

Hall, D. (1999) 'Destination branding, niche marketing and national image projection in Central and Eastern Europe', *Journal of Vacation Marketing* 5(3): 227–37.

Hatch, M. J. and Schultz, M. (1997) 'Relations between organisational culture, identity and image', *European Journal of Marketing* 31(5–6): 356–65.

Ho, W. and Law, W. (2003) 'Education and society in Japan and the People's Republic of China: Comparative perspectives on national identity and national symbols', *Political Crossroads* 10–11: 63–79.

Ji, L. J., Nisbett, R. E. and Su, Y. (2001) 'Culture, change, and prediction', *Psychological Science* 12(6): 450–56.

Kedourie, E. (1992) *Nationalism*, 4th edn, Oxford: Blackwell.

Lee, J. A. (1966) 'Cultural analysis in overseas operations', *Harvard Business Review* March –April: 106–14.

Lessem, R. (1998) *Management Development through Cultural Diversity*, London: Routledge.

Li, P. (1998) 'Towards a geocentric framework of organizational form: A holistic, dynamic and paradoxical approach', *Organization Studies* 19(5): 829–61.

Li, R. (2010) 'Book review – China: the Pessoptimist Nation', *Times Higher Education Supplement*, online, available at: http://www.timeshighereducation.co.uk/story.asp?storyCode=412214&sectioncode=26 (accessed 26 March 2012).

McGregor, T. (2011) 'Fake "Jasmine Revolution" photos expose Western media', online, available at: http://bbs.chinadaily.com.cn/viewthread.php?gid=2&tid=696424 (accessed 4 December 2012).

Marist Poll (2011) online, available at: http://maristpoll.marist.edu/71-independence-day-dummy-seventeen-seventy-when/ (accessed 26 March 2012).

Meissner, W. (2006) 'China's search for cultural and national identity from the nineteenth century to the present', *China Perspectives* 68(November–December), online, available at: http://chinaperspectives.revues. org/3103> (accessed 4 December 2012).

Nation Brand Index (2009) online, available at: http://www.simonanholt.com/Research/research-introduction.aspx (accessed 26 March 2012).

New York Times (2010) online, available at: http://www.nytimes.com/2010/12/10/world/asia/10iht-letter.html (accessed 4 December 2012).

Olins, W. (1999) *Corporate identity: Making business strategy visible through design*, Boston: Harvard Business School Press.

—— (2001a) 'The image of Spain', online, available at: http://www.wallyolins.com/includes/spain.pdf (accessed 26 March 2012).

—— (2001b) 'Poland and national identity', online, available at: http://www.wallyolins.com/includes/poland.pdf (accessed 26 March 2012).

—— (2002) 'Branding the nation – the historical context', *Journal of Brand Management* 9(4–5): 241–8.

Onkvisit, S. and Shaw, J. J. (2008) *International Marketing: Strategy and theory*, 5th edn, New York: Routledge.

Osgood, C. E. and Richards, M. M. (1973) 'From Yang and Yin to and or but', *Language* 49(2): 380–412.

Pye, L. W. (1972) *China: An introduction*, Boston: Little, Brown.

Smith, A. D. (1992) 'National identity and the idea of European identity', *International Affairs* 68(1): 55–76.

Smith, A. D. (1995) 'The formations of national identity', in Harris, H. (ed.) *Identity*, Oxford: Oxford University Press.

Tajfel, H. (1974) 'Social identity and intergroup behaviour', *Social Science Information* 13: 65–93.

Tang, L., Morrison, A. M., Lehto, X. Y., Kline, S. and Pearce, P. L. (2009) 'Effectiveness criteria for icons as tourist attractions: A comparative study between the United States and China', *Journal of Travel & Tourism* 26: 284–302.

Tomlinson, J. (2003) 'Globalisation and cultural identity', online, available at: http://www.polity.co.uk/global/pdf/GTReader2eTomlinson.pdf (accessed 26 March 2012).

Triandafyllidou, A. (1998) 'National identity and the "other"', *Ethnic and Racial Studies*, 21(4): 593–612.

Wanta, W., Golan, G. and Lee, C. (2004) 'Agenda setting and international news: Media influence on public perceptions of foreign nations', *Journalism and Mass Communication Quarterly* 81(2): 364–77.

5 Corporate brand integration in mergers and acquisitions

Joachim Kernstock and
Tim Oliver Brexendorf

Introduction

Most of the academic research on brand management focuses on stable organisational conditions. In the last years, markets have been characterised by disruptive changes as well as mergers and acquisition (M&A) activities. In cases of mergers and acquisitions, the question of choosing an appropriate brand strategy arises. The question of corporate brand identity is a key factor in ensuring a successful M&A outcome (Balmer and Dinnie 1999; Melewar and Harrold 2000; Bahadir et al. 2008; Knowles et al. 2011). Nevertheless, the role of brands is of different importance in M&As. Bahadir et al. (2008) report that 49 per cent of the firm value related to the purchase of Gillette was attributed to the equity of brands whereas in the acquisition of Latitude by Cisco System only 1.51 per cent was attributed to the brand (Bahadir et al. 2008). In M&As, brands are critical assets and often account for significant overall transaction value (Bahadir et al. 2008).

In research and practice little attention has been paid to the external benefits and brand management of mergers (Homburg and Bucerius 2005; Basu 2006). Some authors highlight the relevance of corporate visual identity (Rosson and Brooks 2004), brand name and brand logo integration (Knowles et al. 2011), and customer reactions to M&As (Thorbjornsen and Dahlen 2011). Especially, the integration of brands in M&As is widely neglected in the management of M&As. Articles that discuss possible corporate brand strategies in M&As are scarce (Brockdorff and Kernstock 2001; Ettenson and Knowles 2006; Jaju et al. 2006). This is surprising because it has been reported that many mergers fail because of neglecting the brand integration process. Balmer and Dinnie (1999) argue that the merger failure can be attributed to the fact that a narrow focus on financial issues exists, and crucial issues like corporate brand identity and corporate communication are neglected (Balmer and Dinnie 1999). Illia (2010) states that identity is often undervalued in management practice. Homburg and Bucerius (2005) pronounce that during the integration phase of M&As, managerial tasks are absorbed internally, which can lead to a neglect of the customer and brand perspective.

By merging companies, firms are involved in numerous demanding tasks of integration. One is the integration of corporate and product brands of both companies.

Despite the importance, in practice often little attention is devoted to the integration of brands. Ettenson and Knowles (2006) found that in nearly two-thirds of deals, brand strategy was of low priority in pre-merger discussions. Sometimes the new brand is set almost in a short action prior to the announcement of the merger. In other cases, the issue of brand integration is neglected in the process of post-merger integration. As a consequence, the existing brand values may not be used or may even be destroyed.

The objective of our article is to contribute to the understanding of the integration process of brands in M&As. This article discusses alternative strategic options of brand strategies within a merger. We develop a framework that considers branding options in M&As. We further describe the importance of brand analysis and brand integration strategies in M&As.

Brand management and M&As

Mergers and acquisitions are an integral and indispensable part of today's economic activity (Capron 1999). The reasons for M&As are diverse (Balmer and Dinnie 1999). The intended benefits of M&As are either internal or external. M&As provide an important strategic option for firms to realise internal benefits by expected cost-based synergies and savings (Capron 1999; Knowles *et al.* 2011). External rationales for M&As can be seen in growth and market-entry advantages in increased competition and revenue-based synergies (Capron 1999; Basu 2006).

From a brand-specific perspective, M&As can be brand-intended or non brand-intended. In brand-intended M&As, the acquisition of the brand(s) is a major motivation for the acquisition of the company. In the takeover negotiations regarding the British car producer Rolls-Royce between Volkswagen AG and BMW AG, the brand name Rolls-Royce played the decisive role. M&As which are intended to acquire a brand provide the opportunity to expand the existing brand portfolio and open up new market segments. In brand-intended M&As, mostly a detailed analysis of the brands to be acquired is done. The status of the brands and their role in the strategy of the acquiring company is the main driver for both the decision and the purchase price of the company. In non-brand-intended M&As, the realisation of potential synergies between the acquiring company and the company to be acquired, the acquisition of customers, and the acquisition of know-how are of importance. The acquisition of the brand is often just a side effect. Corporate mergers, which are solely focused on the exploitation of synergies and acquisitions of a customer base, often neglect the market-driven integration of acquired brands. For brand-intended M&As, decisions affecting the brands are often made too late, even left out or not discussed at all in the M&A process. Brand decisions are sometimes made in haste and do not sufficiently consider the long-term effects of the brand decisions. In non-brand-intended M&As, decisions on the continuation or elimination of brands are often influenced by manager preferences of the acquiring company and are unbalanced in the sense that the acquiring company is larger and/or more influential than the target company (Thorbjornsen and Dahlen 2011; Basu 2006). The strategic fit between the brands that need to be integrated and the synergies often play a neglected role. A detailed analysis of the brands and the entire brand portfolio often does not take place and, if it does, is driven by ad hoc management activities.

Brand analysis

As part of the brand analysis in brand-intended M&As, it is intended to evaluate the attractiveness and value of brands to be acquired. In non-brand-intended M&As, the brand analysis provides the basis for the decision of the brand integration. The non-brand-intended M&As are often dominated by the financial perspective of the merger. Balance sheet and financial performance ratios are essential for the company valuation; however, they only reflect a company-based perspective without taking a direct market and customer perspective into account.

In a detailed brand analysis, it is important to evaluate the current and future potential of the brand and the brand portfolio. Understanding the existing and future potential of a brand is critical in terms of corporate strategy and brand

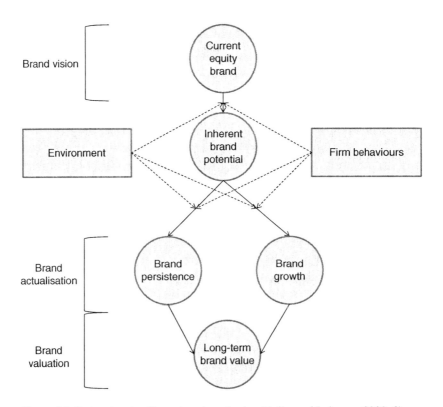

Figure 5.1 Determinants of long-term brand value (Keller and Lehmann 2009: 8)

investment decisions (Keller and Lehmann 2009). Before taking a decision about the future continuation of brands, their current brand equity and value should be analysed. To manage brands within M&As activities properly, the firms should have a clear understanding of the equity of the merged brands. Keller and Lehmann (2009) developed a framework which describes the determinants of long-term brand potential.

Their framework includes the vision of the brand as the inherent potential value of the brand, which is partly based on the current brand equity. The current brand equity is a key in developing a brand vision for the brand(s). The inherent brand potential of the brand reflects what brand value could become in future. The question is, if the inherent brand potential can be transferred into a long-term brand value. The brand needs to be persistent and should allow growth in terms of market penetration, market development and product/services development. This is only possible if the environment and the firm behaviour supports this development (Keller and Lehmann 2009). Besides the future potential of brands, they manifest their value on different levels that need to be considered in the brand analysis – the customer market, the product/services market, and the financial market (Keller and Lehmann 2006). As such, several levels of analysis exist:

Customer level

There are several approaches and key performance indicators to measure the performance of a brand from a customer perspective. Keller and Lehmann (2006) pronounce that the customer-level brand equity can largely be captured by five aspects:

- awareness (ranging from recognition to recall);
- associations (encompassing the tangible and intangible product and service considerations);
- attitude (ranging from acceptability to attraction);
- attachment (ranging from loyalty to addiction);
- activity (including purchase and consumption frequency and involvement with the marketing programme, other customers through word of mouth, etc., or the company).

There are several techniques and tools marketers can use to measure each of these levels.

Product market level

To evaluate brands on the product market level, measures like price premiums, brands' sensitivity towards competitor prices, the ability to maintain and secure distribution channels, etc. should be considered in order to evaluate the brands (Hoeffler and Keller 2003).

Financial market level

From a financial perspective, brands are assets that can be bought or sold. The worth of a brand is therefore the price it could bring on the financial market (Keller and Lehmann 2006). Therefore, the financial market level of measuring brand performance plays an important role in M&As. Over the years, several theoretical as well as practical approaches to evaluate the financial value of a brand have been developed. Salinas and Ambler (2009) give a detailed overview of the existing financial brand evaluation methods.

Furthermore, it is important to understand and analyse the dependencies and interactions of the brands within the brand portfolio and architecture. The brand architecture structures brands on corporate and product brand level. Considering the existing brand architecture is important to integrate the merged brands.

Brand integration strategies in M&As

M&As are disruptive events that imply a discontinuation of the status quo and lead to a fundamental reassessment of the customer's relationship with the brands and their new merged identity (Thorbjornsen and Dahlen 2011; Mizik *et al.* 2011) as well as to a new relationship between the brands themselves. M&As are incidents outside the control of the consumer that may influence their relationship and behaviour towards the brands. Therefore, companies undergoing M&As are faced with the risk of losing customers in M&As (Thorbjornsen and Dahlen 2011). A clear brand strategy is important for managing consumer perceptions based on the strategic intent of the M&A as well as motivating internal stakeholders like employees to align their efforts (Basu 2006; Balmer and Greyser 2002). The main task of brand management in the context of M&As is a sound decision about the acquisition, the continuation, the deletion of existing brands or the creation of new brands. The goal of brand integration is to transfer the pre-existing brand equity into the future and to skim off the equity for the new company. Building brand equity is costly and time intensive (Keller 1993). Therefore, the new brand architecture has to consider the heritage and equity of the merged corporate brands (Muzellec and Lambkin 2008).

A systematic and integrated approach allows increasing brand value, along with shareholder value, and is an inseparable part of the merger integration process (Yang *et al.* 2011). There are several brand integration strategies available (see Figure 5.2). When two companies merge, or one is acquired by another one, a common – possibly a new – corporate brand has to be found. In M&As, the brand strategy should take corporate and product brands into account. The strategies differ in the degree to which the brands of the merging companies remain or will be eliminated and distinguish strategies that maintain both the original brand names (synergistic strategies) and those that do not (dominant and non-synergistic strategies) (Basu 2006; Jaju *et al.* 2006).

The first option, new brand strategy or non-synergistic redeployment, is that both previous corporate brands will be replaced by an entirely new developed

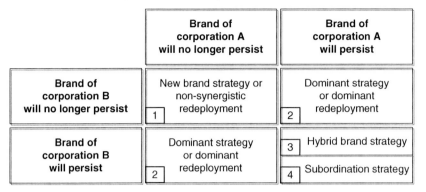

	Brand of corporation A will no longer persist	Brand of corporation A will persist
Brand of corporation B will no longer persist	New brand strategy or non-synergistic redeployment `1`	Dominant strategy or dominant redeployment `2`
Brand of corporation B will persist	Dominant strategy or dominant redeployment `2`	`3` Hybrid brand strategy `4` Subordination strategy

Figure 5.2 Brand strategies in mergers and acquisitions

corporate brand. The development and use of a new corporate brand is appropriate if none of the existing brands has a clear market positioning and do not satisfy the future needs of the customers. Disadvantages of this strategy are the loss of existing corporate brand equity (Jaju *et al.* 2006) and the costs of developing and communicating a new corporate brand.

The second option, the dominant brand strategy or dominant redeployment, is to use one of the two brands as future corporate brand and to give up the second corporate brand. This is often the case in an acquirer-dominant strategy. An example for this strategy is the acquisition of Compaq through Hewlett-Packard. Hewlett-Packard was the new firm name at the expense of the Compaq brand. The acquiring firm keeps the identity and brand name of the acquired firm as a division or subsidiary of the new firm (Jaju *et al.* 2006). Another example is the disappearance of the brands of US-based banks Payne Webber and Warburg Dillon Read after their takeover by UBS, a Swiss bank, after a short transition period. However, internally, their corporate identity and heritage survived in at least one out of three business units.

The third option, the hybrid brand strategy, is a merger of both corporate brand names. Daimler and Chrysler used the hybrid brand strategy and used the hybrid corporate brand name DaimlerChrysler after the merger. More recently this option has been widely used in takeovers within the financial industry: the German Bank Hypovereinsbank operates with the corporate logo of its Italian mother Unicredit. German Commerzbank uses the corporate logo of former Dresdner Bank which, since 2011, has been fully integrated within Commerzbank. Swiss bank Credit Suisse uses the canvas symbol, the corporate logo of US-based investment bank First Boston.

The fourth option, subordinate brand strategy or pure synergistic (non-concatenated) redeployment, is to keep both brands. One is used as the new corporate brand while the other is anchored at the product level. The acquiring firm keeps the identity and brand name of the acquired firm as a division or subsidiary of the new firm (Jaju *et al.* 2006).

The motives for companies choosing a specific option are mostly unclear. The decision depends on the decisions of the executive team (Jaju *et al.* 2006). Research on M&A activities has identified some criteria that are relevant in the context of mergers and acquisitions. Jaju *et al.* (2006) highlight the relevance of brand familiarity, perceived fit and attitude towards the corporate brand as relevant criteria to be considered. More analytical judgment, the measurement of the brand knowledge of the customer or measurement of brand knowledge (Keller 1993) and brand commitment by the employees (Thomson *et al.* 1999) is usually neglected – not to mention an in-depth analysis of the strength of corporate heritage and corporate culture and its relevance to the brand equity. Furthermore, brands are often deeply rooted in the culture of firms and their structures, which indicates high organisational complexity (Capron and Hulland 1999). As such, it is important to appropriately evaluate the value of the brands and to manage the brands of the new brand architecture after transfer in order to capitalise on the brand value (Kapferer 2008).

A case study of corporate brand integration

In a case study of a merger of two Swiss retailers (Kernstock and Brexendorf 2012), one of the authors was embedded within the M&A process alongside the senior management team. The research lends itself to an in-depth study of the brand integration process. The major task of the merger was to find an answer to the question: What is the definite brand architecture for shops of retailer A (premium assortment) and retailer B (mid-range assortment)? The core topic of this process is to elaborate which brand strategy fits best to external market needs and internal cultural and leadership challenges. In the pre-merger situation, there are two established brands with two different business models. In the post-merger situation there will be an additional new future business model, drawing on the existing two business models and, for a limited period of time, the two established businesses will be run in parallel. In the case of the retailers, it will be important to give a pleasurable shopping experience to those consumers who bought at either or both of the merged retailers.

Retailer A was established in 1993 as a wholesale cooperative without branding to customers. At the end of the 1990s the firm started branding its products and services under a corporate brand. The assortment of the retailer is premium priced. Brand awareness and brand preference of customers has been continuously measured and significantly leveraged over the past five years. The retailer is confronted with an intensive competitive environment among major suppliers. Most of the 150 outlets are not high-frequency locations.

Retailer B is a small retailer established in 1975 as a wholesale cooperative with a mid-range assortment. The retail brand has been communicated to its customers since its foundation. Brand awareness and brand preference has been continuously tracked. However, it was significantly weaker than that of company A by the time of this merger process. Retailer B has half as many outlets as retailer A. However, most of its outlets are in high-frequency high street locations.

In this specific case the solution for the future brand architecture is structured as follows. The outlets of retailer A will run with corporate brand A in the future to save its premium brand positioning. The outlets of B will run with corporate brand B to save its more economic positioning and access to mid-range mass assortments. A new business model with an enhanced customer experience, comprising premium and mid-range assortments and new-to-market special customer services is a major result of the merger process. The competitive advantage of the new business model is the integrated range of assortments combined with an attractive service portfolio, not fast and easy to copy by competitors. The future business model will be run under brand A. The new business model should benefit from the premium positioning of retailer A, its higher brand awareness and brand preference. Furthermore, the transition process for outlets of retailer A into the new business model will be supported by the benefits of the new service innovations and improved customer experience. Those outlets of retailer B which are converted into the new business model then participate in the new services and have a rationale for leveraging their assortment. In the final phase, most of retailer A will be converted into the new business model. Outlets of retailer B which are not converted can run their establishment with the more economic mid-range brand B. For future new outlets there are two options to choose: Full size and service under premium brand A or economic mid-size brand B. Each brand has a specific perspective for its development under one roof. No brand equity is diluted (see Table 5.1).

Why is there no new brand for the new business model? The management decisions are based on the following arguments: (1) Saving an expensive new brand launch; the critical mass for a successful brand launch will not be reached by the merger process. (2) Migration process over all shops into the new business model will take years. (3) Service innovations should be used to strengthen the positive success track of brand A. (4) The more powerful participants of this merger process want to see their brand in the marketplace in the future. This argument supports the view that the new brand architecture is often an outcome of a

Table 5.1 Entities and corporate brand architecture

Entities	Retailer A	New business model to be launched after merger	Retailer B
Current brand architecture	Corporate Brand A (Premium assortment oriented)	Not yet on market	Corporate Brand B (Mid-range assortment oriented)
Future brand architecture	Corporate Brand A (Premium assortment, brand vividness supported by new business model)	Corporate Brand A (Premium assortment, brand vividness supported by new business model)	Corporate Brand B (Targeting on mass market)

political process. Nevertheless, brand perspective supports a content-driven merger moderation process and all arguments underline the importance of a comprehensive view of the brand architecture in an M&A process from the very beginning. Table 5.2 highlights the observation in action research and suggests that the brand integration process is able to balance the influential power relations in M&As and shift political discussions to a more content-oriented level of decision quality.

The results of this case study demonstrate the growing importance of brand integration in M&As. This poses a real challenge to the managements of the acquiring and the target firms alike. To make use of the growth potential, it is of high importance to expose and emphasise the brand perspective of M&As. A detailed brand analysis that considers the financial brand value and brand

Table 5.2 Structure of project and action research observations

Project subgroup	Role in merger process	Observation in action research
Corporate brand management and project steering	Leading project group with full board member attention; responsible for new business model and assortment decision making	Political power play overrules market data. Brand perspective supports content-driven merger moderation process
Marketing planning	Operative road to market	Based on brand management decisions
Assortment/Category management	Responsible for synergy development	Key relevance for new business model; brand architecture decisions are based on rigour data
Wholesale dealers and partnerships	Responsible for synergy development	Key relevance for new business model; decisions based on political agenda
Training and human resource management	Responsible for new business perspectives and implementation of new services of new business model	Based on brand management decisions. Employee/customer experience is key for new business model
IT-Infrastructure	Consolidation and merger of IT-database and POS client management	Part of post-merger integration
Quality	Implementations of service quality	Key reference for new business model
Structure	Development of new corporate centre after merger	Decision based on political agenda
Tax and legal	Implementation of merger process into agreement level	Not part of observation and action research process

equity, the relationship between brands and their positioning should be done in any M&A process. For the integration of corporate brands four different strategies are available which can be used to preserve the brand value from the past or ideally enhance it. The findings of the case study show that in practice decisions regarding the brand portfolio and the post-merger brand architecture are mainly based on political power play and not comprehensive judgment of brand equity data. Nevertheless, the brand perspective should be integrated in an M&A process starting with the pre-merger phase onwards. Furthermore, the process of developing a common and future brand strategy can play a deal-making role in sending signals inside and outside the organisation.

References

Bahadir, S. C., Bharadwaj, S. G. and Srivastava, R. K. (2008) 'Financial value of brands in mergers and acquisitions: Is value in the eye of the beholder?', *Journal of Marketing* 72(November): 49–64.

Balmer, J. M. T. and Dinnie, K. (1999) 'Merger madness: The final coup de grâce', *Journal of General Management* 24(4): 53–70.

Balmer, J. M. T. and Greyser, S. A. (2002) 'Managing the multiple identities of the corporation', *California Management Review* 44(3): 72–86.

Basu, K. (2006) 'Merging brands after mergers', *California Management Review* 48(4): 28–40.

Brockdorff, B. and Kernstock, J. (2001) 'Brand Integration Management. Erfolgreiche Markenführung bei Mergers & Akquisitions', *Thexis* 18(4): 54–60.

Capron, L. (1999) 'The long-term performance of horizontal acquisitions', *Strategic Management Journal* 20(11): 987–1018.

Capron, L. and Hulland, J. (1999) 'Redeployment of brands, sales forces, and general marketing management expertise following horizontal acquisitions: A resource-based view', *Journal of Marketing* 63(April): 41–54.

Ettenson, R. and Knowles, J. (2006) 'Merging the brands and branding the merger', *MIT Sloan Management Review* 47(4): 38–49.

Gotsi, M. and Andriopoulos, C. (2007) 'Understanding the pitfalls in the corporate rebranding process', *Corporate Communications: An international journal* 14(4): 341–55.

Hoeffler, S. and Keller, K. L. (2003) 'Building strong brands', *Journal of Brand Management* 10(6): 421–45.

Homburg, C. and Bucerius, M. (2005) 'A marketing perspective on mergers and acquisitions: How marketing integration affects post merger performance', *Journal of Marketing* 69(1): 95–113.

Illia, L. (2010) 'How business disciplines discuss multiple identities in organisations', *Corporate Reputation Review* 12(4): 327–44.

Jaju, A., Joiner, C. and Reddy, S. K. (2006) 'Consumer evaluations of corporate brand redeployments', *Journal of the Academy of Marketing Science* 34(2): 206–15.

Kapferer, J. N. (2008) *The new strategic brand management: creating and sustaining brand equity long term*, London: Kogan Page.

Keller, K. L. (1993) 'Conceptualizing, measuring, and managing customer-based brand equity', *Journal of Marketing* 57(1): 1–22.

Keller, K. L. and Lehmann, D. (2006) 'Brands and branding: Research findings and future priorities', *Marketing Science* 25 (November/December): 740–59.

82 *Joachim Kernstock and Tim Oliver Brexendorf*

—— (2009) 'Assessing long-term brand potential', *Journal of Brand Management* 17(1): 6–17.

Kernstock, J. and Brexendorf, T. O. (2012) 'Corporate brand integration in mergers and acquisitions – an action research based approach', *Corporate Reputation Review* 15(3): 169–78.

Knowles, J., Dinner, I. and Mizik, N. (2011) 'Why fusing company identities can add value', *Harvard Business Review* September: 26.

Melewar, T. and Harrold, J. (2000) 'The role of corporate identity systems in merger and acquisition activity', *Journal of General Management* 26(2): 17–31.

Mizik, N., Knowles, J. and Dinner, I. (2011) 'Value implications of corporate branding in mergers', working paper, online, available at: http://papers.ssrn.com/sol3/papers.cfm?abstract_id=1756368 (accessed 22 November 2012).

Muzellec, L. and Lambkin, M. (2008) 'Corporate rebranding and the implications for brand architecture management: the case of Guinness (Diageo) Ireland', *Journal of Strategic Marketing* 16(4): 283–99.

Rosson, P. and Brooks, M. R. (2004) 'M&As and corporate visual identity', *Corporate Reputation Review* 7(2): 181–94.

Salinas, G. and Ambler, T. (2009) 'A taxonomy of brand valuation practice: methodologies and purposes', *Journal of Brand Management* 17(1): 39–61.

Thomson, K., de Chernatony, L., Arganbright, L. and Khan, S. (1999) 'The buy-in benchmark: how staff understanding and commitment impact brand and business performance', *Journal of Marketing Management* 15(8): 819–35.

Thorbjornsen, H. and Dahlen, M. (2011) 'Customer reactions to acquirer-dominant mergers and acquisitions', *International Journal of Research in Marketing* 28: 332–41.

Vallaster, C. (2004) 'Internal brand building in multicultural organisations: a roadmap towards action research', *Qualitative market research: an international journal* 7(2): 100–113.

Yang, D., Davis, D. A. and Robertson, K. R. (2011) 'Integrated branding with mergers and acquisitions', *Journal of Brand Management* 19: 438–56.

Part 2

An employee perspective to brand and identity management

6 Relationships and quality management

The Pastificio Rana case study

*Emanuele Invernizzi and
Stefania Romenti*

That communication has taken on a strategic role in governance and organisational development is now widely accepted among communication and management scholars (Argenti 2008; Cornelissen 2011; van Riel and Fombrun 2007). This thesis is reinforced by pointing out that the process of institutionalising communication, which began at the end of the twentieth century, has firmly established itself in large firms, both public and private.

The institutionalisation of communication occurs through several processes, which clearly demonstrate its growing presence in businesses. For example, the head of communications becomes Chief Communication Officer; this person becomes part of the executive committee and increasingly participates in the most important strategic decisions of the company. Further support of the growing strategic role of communication in the governance and success of companies – beyond that of its institutionalisation – can be found by demonstrating how communication has become a core element of business activity. To this end, the entrepreneurial communication paradigm (Invernizzi and Romenti 2009; 2013) has been developed in order first to interpret and second to illustrate how and to what extent communication is used to support strategic business development.

In the first part of this chapter we review the institutional theory and entrepreneurial organisation theory (EOT) and we discuss their potential for interpreting the strategic role that communication is called to play within complex organisations. In the second part, we describe the Pastificio Rana case study of an Italian company that produces fresh pasta. The company was established in 1961 and in a few years became a very successful multinational corporation. The founder and current President, Giovanni Rana, has always made use of principles based primarily on communicational and relational tools to govern his company and to lead it to success. We will illustrate how Giovanni Rana has always carefully considered the communicational and relational aspects of any kind of strategic and operating decision-making process. Finally, we will analyse and discuss the case study in the light of the institutionalisation and entrepreneurial organisational theory of the firm, describing the particular strategic roles communication has played in the success of the firm.

What does the entrepreneurial theory of the firm tell us in terms of the strategic role of communication within organisations?

It may seem paradoxical, but for an organisation to be successful, it must be in line with the values of the society in which it operates (as held in the institutionalisation theory), yet at the same time stand out, especially through the creative and innovative processes of its own distinctive resources (as contended in the resource-based view of the firm). In other words, to achieve success, a company must maintain a delicate balance between isomorphism and differentiation.

Isomorphism

According to the theories of institutionalism and new institutionalism, the survival and success of business organisations is related to their capacity for accepting and adopting the dominant values of the environment in which they operate as the fundamental guideline in their way of being and of acting. By adopting values that are homogeneous with the context, organisations become institutions (Selznick 1948, 1957) and acquire the level of public acceptance necessary for success (Meyer and Rowan 1977).

Adopting the guiding principles that prevail in society is particularly important for business organisations because it gives them the seal of approval to act in that social context and stimulates cohesion and involvement of those who are part of the organisations themselves. To recognise those principles, state them clearly, propose them to the organisation's top management and, finally, propagate them within the organisation itself is an important part of the role of public relations and corporate communication.

That role has been defined as strategic-reflective (van Ruler and Vercic 2002): it is strategic because of the strategic importance of adopting such guiding values and because of the high level in the organisation that the role itself aims at; it is reflective, because it analyses the prevailing social values and works to 'reflect' them into the organisation from the outside.

Differentiation

On the other hand, organisations should be oriented to differentiation. They must be able to create, maintain and spread the distinctive resources that make them competitive. The potential of such resources must be identified and evaluated; from there, the strategy that best reinforces their application should be selected. First, out of the pool of tacit skills already existing in the organisation, the distinctive skills must be identified by making them explicit and by combining them. Second, they must then be made available to all members of the organisation.

According to the dynamic capability theory (Teece and Pisano 1994), successful business organisations possess the dynamic capacity to coordinate innovation effectively and flexibly, and to adapt, integrate and reconfigure internal resources and skills. The role that communication experts can play in key relational processes is crucial. It entails the communicational and relational skills of those involved in all the processes of identification, qualification and propagation of knowledge as well as of the company's distinctive resources. It also has to do with the strictly operational skills of the role of PR/CC, defined as formative and consultative.

A paradox

The entrepreneurial organisation theory (Álvarez and Barney 2004; Burns 2005; Busenitz *et al.* 2003; Bygrave 1989; Dew *et al.* 2004; Foss and Klein 2005; Ireland *et al.* 2003) provides a unique conceptual framework that serves to integrate and enhance each strategic need for the success of organisations. On the one hand, companies need to be aligned with the external context in order to obtain a licence to operate (isomorphism). In contrast, they also need to create distinctive competences in order to be competitive (differentiation). Entrepreneurial organisation theories (EOTs) are based on five main pillars: gate-keeping; networking; orientation to innovation; transformative leadership; enactment.

Gate-keeping consists of gathering continuously updated outside information and knowledge regarding areas of interest for organisational development. This may include introducing technological innovation or initiating change in the market or within the organisational environment. Strategic communication, through its aligning and boundary function, holds an advantageous position for observing and interpreting an organisation's operational context. This is considered a central theme in strategic management studies to guarantee long-term corporate survival.

Networking favours the development, maintenance and improvement of internal communication networks to support work groups, and favours the development and cultivation of relationships and alliances that are entrepreneurial keys for ideas, information, advice and resources needed to survive. Strategic communication's main goal consists of building bridges between the organisation and its most important stakeholders, as well as activating and facilitating the participation and involvement of company members.

Orientation to innovation is a vital dimension of entrepreneurial theory. This means to identify new opportunities and markets, to evaluate potentialities and ideas. Innovative ability should be developed within organisations, so that it is not concentrated in a few individuals. It requires both broad and specific knowledge of techniques and managerial practices. Strategic communication can be a precious support of innovation when its main goal is to create a collaborative culture and fertile climate. To foster innovation and changes, communication should support management in reassuring employees regarding changes, supplying adequate information and, in particular, listening to what happens inside the organisational context (Zerfass and Huck 2007).

Transformative leadership is fundamental to developing and using the innovative ability that is generated within organisations. This means knowing how to unfold innovative potential in an organisation, overcome critical obstacles, and resolve any opposition through constant search for commitment on the part of key stakeholders. Entrepreneurial organisation theory stresses the importance of formulating a vision of the project, thus encouraging organisational members to actively support the project and developing a relationship of trust and respect with every one of them. Communication plays a strategic role in developing transformative leadership and vision. Communicating strategic company decisions serves to channel collective energy to a common goal. In the case of external stakeholders, strategic communication activities are essential to both shaping a single, clear company position in the minds of its stakeholders and developing a solid long-term reputation (Cornelissen 2011). These studies stress the importance of combining all communication activities so as to ensure the coherence of messages and the strategic intent of the organisation (van Riel 1995).

Enactment: the entrepreneurial organisation carries out a process of enactment, a term used to indicate a process of activation and creation of the environment on the basis of individual interpretation to which meaning is attributed (Daft and Weick 1984; Weick 1995). In this case, communication becomes something more than an infrastructural component of the business. Scholars who define the theories of communication as constitutive of the organisation (Putnam and Nicotera 2009; Reed 2010; Sewell 2010) base their theories on Weick's (1995) concept of organisational sense-making, according to which reality is created through a cognitive process of interpretation rooted in individual mental maps. An organisation is seen as a continuous product constantly transforming the communicative actions of its members (Bisel 2010; Cooren *et al.* 2006; Kuhn, 2008). In the next sections, the components of the entrepreneurial organisation theory and the strategic dimensions of communication will be used to interpret the path to success of Pastificio Rana.

The Pastificio Rana case study

In this section, we investigate the case of a company which was built by Giovanni Rana and it is based on a paradox: he invented a product, tortellini, which already existed. The only difference between the old and the new product was that the tortellini that Giovanni Rana envisioned was an industrial product, while the existing one was a traditional home-made dish or, perhaps, a handcrafted product sold in small local shops. Giovanni Rana started as a craftsman himself, having had in mind a clear idea: to produce high-quality tortellini on a large scale. The tortellini were to be not just as good as the home-made ones but even better, for at least two reasons: the high quality of the ingredients, and the consistent quality of the product.

Early history

Giovanni was born in Cologna Veneta, in the province of Verona, on 15 October 1937, the last of seven children. His brother Francesco began work as a baker and bread maker; Giovanni later followed in his footsteps. It was this early experience that laid the foundation of Giovanni's future as an entrepreneur in the sector of fresh pasta and tortellini, a type of ring-shaped stuffed pasta. Giovanni first made bread with his brothers and then began to personally look after the distribution, dedicating himself to both activities with passion and lively curiosity. While delivering bread, he especially took advantage of the opportunity to observe and talk with the people he dealt with; this experience formed the basis of the inspiration for his first fresh pasta creations. Giovanni defined this activity as home-made marketing, comprised above all of personally contacting and listening to his clients in order to understand their needs, which he then transformed into experimentation and finally innovation.

At the end of the 1950s, Giovanni announced that he wanted to dedicate himself to the production of tortellini. This innovative idea arose out of the intuition of a brand new trend in consumption patterns. Giovanni's insight referred to the steady increase in the number of women who worked outside of the home. This was a change in lifestyle that had significantly modified the role of women, who now had less time to spend on household activities.

It follows that, in the food sector, there was expanded opportunity for producing and marketing products that could be prepared in less time, yet kept the characteristics and quality of dishes traditionally made from scratch at home. Giovanni's insight was further strengthened by his choice of product; tortellini is a food that is rich in terms of both taste and symbolic value, and that lends itself to infinite variations on the basic theme. Giovanni realised that the change and the possibility of success lay in finding a formula that allowed him to make a long-standing handcrafted product on an industrial scale, but one that at the same time maintained its link to traditional quality.

In 1961, little more than a year after his decision to start up the tortellini production, Giovanni opened his own pasta factory, which was no more than an artisanal workshop. Success came rapidly and, in the wake of increasing demand, the workshop became bigger and better organised. Initially, production was entirely handcrafted, it was limited to only one type of tortellini, with a meat filling, and the tortellini was produced exclusively to order. Within three years, production had increased to the point that it became necessary to build a larger facility equipped with a mechanised production line that made it possible to make the transition from artisanal to industrial and achieve a substantial leap in productivity. This was the moment at which Giovanni had to face a genuine quality dilemma: how could he guarantee his customers tortellini at the same level of quality as the traditional handmade pasta, even though it was produced by machine?

Innovation and attention to quality

The way that Giovanni faced and resolved the dilemma was emblematic of the approach to quality and innovation found in Pastificio Rana. At that time, the only machine available on the market was able to produce a ring-shaped tortellino and was fitted with a continuous threaded screw device to put the filling in the tortellino.

As this was unsuitable for the home-made kind of tortellino Giovanni had in mind, he asked for specific modifications to the machine.

With the first modification, the round pasta became triangular, making it possible to hand-finish the product, thus achieving a tortellino similar to a home-made shape. With the second modification, the threaded screw device was replaced by a type of plunger. In this way, the filling was not crushed and maintained its original consistency, just like hand-filled pasta.

The importance of the two changes lay in the resulting perception of the finished product, both visually – the folded tortellino had the same appearance as a home-made one – and also in terms of palate, since the filling also had the same consistency as home-made. The modified machinery allowed Rana to produce unique fresh pasta, distinct from that of the competition.

Innovation and product durability

The challenge for the company was focused on lengthening the shelf-life of the product so as to be able to increase production. The introduction of pasteurisation in 1968 had made it possible to prolong the life of the product up to ten days. However, over the years, the growth in demand was such that even the possibility of storing the product for ten days began to hamper the potential development of the Pastificio. Once again, Giovanni came up with a unique idea. He observed that sparkling mineral water which contained added carbon dioxide lasted much longer than regular mineral water. Thus he had the idea of using carbon dioxide to preserve the tortellini.

With this innovation, it became possible for Rana products to switch to a new type of packaging, designed for the application of a new method of preservation in plastic bags into which a mixture of carbon dioxide and nitrogen was injected. At the same time, the graphics and the brand logo were renewed. The Rana brand logo was presented as a maker's signature, with the aim of conveying to the consumer that the producer, Giovanni Rana, personally guaranteed the quality of the product.

During the 1980s, with steady growth stabilised at around 20 per cent, Pastificio Rana became the established market leader in Italy. In the same period the process of rationalisation of the entire business was almost completed. At this time, Giovanni's son, Gianluca Rana, who officially entered the firm in 1986, became an important player in the company.

Transformative leadership: sustaining generational synergy

Following a period of gradual integration, Gianluca was ready to take the reins of the company together with his father. In 1991 he was named Director General and CEO of Pastificio Rana. The role of Chairman was retained by Giovanni, who still acts as head of the company, providing general guidelines for the firm and contributing to product development.

Gianluca is in charge of the daily management of the company, a role of para-mount importance in adapting production processes and company structure to the growing challenges posed by internal growth as well as an increasingly competitive external market environment. In describing this management style, one that plans for areas of competence that are well outlined, yet complementary and integrated, Giovanni, when speaking about generational change, likes to define his experience as generational synergy – quite the opposite of what is usually perceived as the generational problem.

It is clear that Giovanni places the highest importance on the relationship with his son; he realises that only with the help of Gianluca, holder of new managerial skills, will it be possible to continue the drive to innovate and grow that is vital to the success of the company. Therefore a considerable part of Giovanni's leadership is devoted to his relationship with Gianluca, to stay by his son's side and help him to grow. Giovanni also pays close attention to adapting commercial policies to the steady rise in large-scale retail trade, a significant trend since the 1980s.

Implementing relations with large-scale retail trade

The growth of large retailers has required a timely adjustment of Pastificio Rana's commercial policies. Relations with these large distribution companies is crucial and has been entrusted to Gianluca Rana, with the aim of cultivating a relationship based on trust with the presidents and CEOs of distribution groups. Negotiating with large retailers also takes place at an international level since the groups have outlets in different countries and increasingly deal only with producers who can export to all the countries in which the groups are present. Therefore, to have a meaningful position in large-scale retail trade in Italy, it is also necessary to be present in the main European countries where the large retailers operate.

The widening of the negotiating territory with the dealers implies an increase in a producer's marketing potential; however, it also requires timely adaptation to a changing situation in order to stay competitive. Pastificio Rana responded to the changes with the RED project (Rana European Development). The project's core objective is to extend the presence of Pastificio Rana into the main European countries by means of a thorough knowledge of the diverse distributive systems of individual countries. In fact, it is the intention of the RED project to bring the dialogue with large retailers to an international level, not just through the export of an Italian product, but also through the development of new products as well as new ways of relating appropriately to the individual European national markets.

Pastificio Rana often invites representatives of large retailers to the Experience Centre, located at the villa owned by the Rana family on Lake Garda, where Gianluca frequently organises evening events. The culinary-themed events are an excellent occasion to field test new recipes and flavours, at the same time paying close attention to relations with customers, journalists and opinion leaders who will in turn speak to others about the Rana style. On these occasions, Gianluca himself, as well as other members of the executive management, dressed as cooks and waiters, prepare and serve dinner to the guests. The primary purpose of these events is commercial, to be sure, but on these occasions a warm atmosphere is created that favours the founding and maintaining of important personal customer relations, both in and out of the company. In fact these evenings are a metaphor for the careful attention to relationships that is such a vital factor in the success of Pastificio Rana. They demonstrate how an awareness of the personal human aspect has always held great significance in Rana's business relations. This value is deeply rooted in the company's history, from its handmade origins right through to the present and the next phase of company growth, in which it has become a key factor in the featured style of Pastificio Rana.

Advertising: implementing relations with customers

Advertising campaigns were introduced by Pastificio Rana in 1987; in 1989 there was a turning point, with a company investment equal to ten per cent of its turnover. From the beginning, traditional advertising campaigns have had the almost exclusive purpose of advertising a product; Giovanni Rana's great innovation was to provide a testimonial for the product, entering into a personal relationship with the consumers. Although differing in content and setting, each one of the adverts sought to position the brand firmly on the quality of the pasta and its link to tradition, with the aim of consolidating Giovanni's commitment to the consumer.

The famous 1990 campaign where, for the first time, Giovanni Rana appeared as a young boy who tries over and over to roll out the pasta for the tortellini, without success, marked a special moment for the company. In this period, many large companies and multinationals, attracted by the profitability of the fresh pasta market, were trying to get into the action, especially through policies of acquisition. One of the main tools chosen by Pastificio Rana to defend its market share was the advertising in which Giovanni himself guaranteed his products, underlining a strong point that made them stand out among all the competitors.

Indeed, his tortellini are a high-quality handcrafted product, linked to a tradition that Giovanni Rana knows deeply as part of his personal history. The first campaigns with Giovanni providing a testimonial were decisive in positioning the brand as shown by the considerable increase in indices of recognition: from 44 per cent in 1990 to 69 per cent in 1993.

In 1997, the 'Hollywood' campaign was launched, in which Giovanni spoke with some of the greatest actors in the history of cinema, who asked him the secret of his pasta *fresca*. Giovanni appeared with Marilyn Monroe, Rita Hayworth and Humphrey Bogart among others. Brand awareness jumped to 90.2 per cent and the successful campaign continued to be shown with numerous variations on the theme up to 2000.

The year 2002 brought the 'Thank you, Giovanni Rana' campaign, a series of commercials where consumers take on a central role, underlining their relation to the maker of the product. The consumers in this series of four commercials express their appreciation for Giovanni Rana's products, each time performing a simple thank you task, such as painting his front gate, cooking for him or washing his car. The key focus of this campaign was to underline both the numerous new pasta *fresca* items as well as the products' high quality. In addition, they expressed appreciation for the approach of the company, personified by Giovanni, towards the customers.

Continuous research and development of new products

Careful attention to the product, typical of Giovanni from the very beginning, can be found in the relevance attributed to R&D and to his research laboratory that aims to introduce new product categories, to extend the range with new tastes and formats and to design continuous improvements to the production cycle.

The research centre is divided into three main areas. The first area concerns the conception of new products, growing out of researchers' intuition or even that of Giovanni or Gianluca themselves. The second area deals with innovation in productive technologies or the introduction of new machinery, perhaps adapting machines from other sectors. An interesting example of the results of process innovation was the creation of the new product line *Sfogliagrezza*. For the first time, a new line of pasta was launched with a slightly rough surface; this feature allows the cooked pasta to better hold the sauce or seasoning.

The third area of innovation is called 'look and taste' and focuses on a continuous daily tasting of new products and flavours coming from all types of food culture, even if not strictly linked to pasta *fresca*. All innovations that emerge from the research centre are screened in the light of corporate strategy before being launched onto the market. All new products must be in line with the guiding principle of being perceived as a Rana product, with the unmistakable features of quality and genuineness that are expected by regular customers of the product. Indeed, the new products are not intended to be merely visually appealing; they must have an authentic quality that differentiates them from other pasta products already on the market, so that they cannot be easily imitated by the competition. Product innovation is therefore one of the keys to understanding how Pastificio Rana has managed to achieve success in the past and maintain a leading position in its sector over time.

Engaging managers and employees

The involvement of people who work for and with the company is another strong point of Pastificio Rana. The origins of the pasta factory, deeply attached to its territory, firmly grounded in craftsmanship and characterised by strong interpersonal relations, are evident in the current style of human resource management. As evidence of the strategic relevance of relations, the role of HR manager is carried out by the current CEO. Gianluca Rana himself deals with the job interviews and final hiring decisions. The selection of new personnel is determined not only by the candidate's skills, but even more by the candidates' attitude to act in accordance with the style of Pastificio. This is an application of a principle renowned for its extensive adoption at the end of the twentieth century by

South West Airlines. This American air carrier states: 'We hire for attitudes, we train for skills', a notion that affirms that the main criteria for selection of new staff should be the sharing of the company's core values.

The relationship between top management and staff emphasises the basic choice, according to which knowledge transfer and problem-solving take place for the most part informally and through unstructured dialogue. This can be found, for example, in an established habit of managers, who meet every morning in front of the coffee machine, located near Gianluca's office, to exchange ideas before starting their working day. This informal means has proved effective in the creation and reinforcement of strong cohesive involvement of staff that goes well beyond the job description of the various company roles.

The pillars of success of Giovanni Rana: adopting the entrepreneurial organisation approach

Like all recipes that lead to the creation of an excellent product, and have enjoyed extraordinary success, the 'recipe' for development of Pastificio Rana has created new pathways.

Enactment: creating a new product

Indeed, during the initial phase, Giovanni seemed driven only by passion and personal intuition when he started up his own production of tortellini. Nevertheless, this decision, so unusual at the time – Giovanni's own family did not understand it – was based on what we could now define as a careful market analysis. Giovanni used tools that we can now readily define as professional, such as in-depth interviews and participant observation, which young Giovanni used even before starting his adventure with pasta *fresca*.

Giovanni defines his early analyses and home-made marketing. In fact, the initial perception of more women working outside the home, as well as the gradual spread of consumption of products that previously had been considered a luxury, was anything but superficial. Rather, it comprised an accurate interpretation of changes in consumer patterns.

It is interesting to note the other considerations that Giovanni made about the product in that early period. For example, that of quality, both real and perceived, took on substance and form in Giovanni's mind even before he started and then, in the very first years of his activity: real quality in the sense that a successful pasta product had to have those superior characteristics that made them the equal of the tortellini that traditional homemakers prepared from scratch with the best ingredients and great care; perceived quality in the sense that the tortellini wasn't only to be produced with good ingredients and adequate production methods in order to be appealing to consumers' taste. In addition, the form of the product and the way it was packaged needed to evoke a sense of home-made or handcrafted; these elements were considered equally important.

In analysing the home-made marketing and product conception that Giovanni was gradually defining, it is possible to isolate some ideas that matured and took shape at the beginning and that would be reinforced and extended in the future, following a path that firmly grounded itself in tradition. The first idea was the potential for development of the market for stuffed pasta. This idea surely derived from observing the increasing difficulty for housewives to make this more elaborate dish (usually reserved for special occasions) themselves. Furthermore, demand for this product was growing as it became available. Thus the product had real specialness given the high quality and variety of its ingredients and symbolic specialness because of its association with festivities and other special occasions when it was traditionally served.

The second idea lay in the focus on high quality, a requisite of all Rana products. This basic premise that Giovanni started with and would never minimise even with the industrial evolution of production methods, is based on the notion that Rana tortellini had to be at least as good as those made at home. In actual fact, they would have to be even better due to the consistent level of high quality that Rana production was able to guarantee. The third idea concerned the potential for the evolution and expansion of tortellini products, able to take their place next to the traditional dish of meat-filled tortellini. Evolution implied a practically infinite series of variations on the original theme. Later production of tortellini would amply demonstrate the feasibility of this idea, which at the beginning was purely based on an intuition to be developed. Nevertheless, Giovanni had foreseen the potential reach of this idea and incorporated it into his initial activity.

Essentially, the tortellini that Giovanni envisioned was a new product in relation to home-made ones; even though they had to possess all the intrinsic and evocative characteristics of home-made tortellini, they had also to move beyond the traditional in terms of constant quality and variety.

Transformative leadership: engaging in quality and growth

The idea of quality, totally shared by Gianluca, continues to be a real obsession for Giovanni, alongside that of production development. The two facets are inseparable in Giovanni's vision and in some ways are even more so in Gianluca's view. The two aspects seem extremely difficult to reconcile; indeed, the real challenge is to combine handcrafted quality with industrial production. One of the main keys to success of Pastificio Rana lies in the continuous innovation applied to productive techniques, aimed at advancing productivity and product durability, while maintaining high levels of quality.

The injecting of carbon dioxide and nitrogen into the package proved successful in increasing the life of the product without altering any of its organoleptic properties (taste and mouth feel for example).Thus, the start-up of production in clean rooms without interruption of the cold chain throughout the entire process of production as well as delivery of the product was highly significant.

This further innovation lengthened the life of the product, reducing the necessity of pasteurisation and eliminating the use of preservatives. The focus on marketing as a driver that is complementary to the quality and variety of the product is certainly another key success factor.

The consistent factor in Rana's business relations at all levels is the scrupulous attention to interpersonal relationships, starting with Gianluca Rana, who maintains relations with the CEOs of large retail multinationals and following with an articulated business structure, able to respond to specific relational demands that may come up at various levels of the distribution chain.

Networking: a relational advertising

Maintaining a direct relationship with customers, as did Giovanni at the beginning – he gave free tortellini to taste to potential customers as his only form of advertising and promotions – grew more complex as the company increased in size. Advertising, therefore, became a necessity, also to hold out against the competition from multinationals, which were making serious inroads into the pasta *fresca* market. This urgent need soon became the platform for another key success factor.

If it is true that Rana's winning strategy is based on quality and innovation applied to his basic creation, achieving an industrial product with distinctive hand-made quality, then it follows that company advertising will make use of the same approach. The first advertisements at the end of the 1980s indeed focused on the product's genuine nature and high-quality ingredients. These ads sought to deliver the message that Rana tortellini were created with the same care that is devoted to a handcrafted product. The strategy didn't change with the long series of TV advertisements in which Giovanni himself appeared to speak about the goodness and quality of the ingredients he used as well as the production methods of his company, which followed the principles of handcrafted production. The advertisements certainly showed a high level of creativity and many of them are memorable even now; for example, the one in which Giovanni appeared with great Hollywood actors or met such historical figures as Stalin, or the one in which he landed on the moon. However, the constant theme of the advertising message remained the same: to reiterate the high quality of the basic ingredients and the production that respected handcrafting traditions. This is advertising that strives to activate and maintain a direct relationship with the customers. The essence of this principle is clearly seen in the series of commercials 'Thank you, Giovanni Rana' in which groups of friends or families of consumers thank Giovanni for his products and express their appreciation by performing small tasks, such as cooking for him, washing his car or painting his garden fence.

Advertising is a crucial success factor inasmuch as it stays strongly linked to the product qualities such as originality, good taste and wholesomeness. This is a far cry from promotional messages linked only to image and imagery so dear to postmodernism. The solid relationship with the customer in advertising (but also in reality) is based, as already mentioned, on the quality of the product itself and the implicit pact between producer and consumer.

Innovation: high-quality new products

With the recent project of a chain of restaurants, a new transformation has happened before our eyes; a real transformation, but above all, a symbolic one, of the tortellini as first course. This takes place in the restaurants, whose kitchens in full operation can be viewed by passers-by in the street, and in the many corner kitchens already in operation, where pasta dishes are prepared in front of the customer. In other words, the element of traditional home hospitality service is enacted in real time in front of the customer. This enactment can be repeated at home with the purchased products: for example, a customer buys the *colpo di fiamma* product, takes it home and mixes it with the fresh sauce that is sold with the pasta product. This is quite a different experience from defrosting a food product or reheating a precooked package of pasta. The idea is to provide the customer with the means of preparing an excellent Italian first course at home, using fresh ingredients and with every possibility of personalising the dish.

Product innovations such as fresh sauces or filled gnocchi (a type of dumpling) were already going in this direction, even before the launch of the product *colpo di fiamma*. The restaurant project, and its parallel partner, the Giovanni Rana Trattorie and the Rana Corners, also symbolically develop the transformation of the fresh pasta product into a fresh first course.

Of course, the aim of these initiatives is to publicise and raise awareness of Rana products, offering them in contrast (especially in the corner kitchens) to the range of fast foods that are found in shopping malls. The other aim, however, is to demonstrate how to prepare a superb traditional Italian first course, with fresh ready-to-use ingredients, whether you are in Italy or not.

Conclusions. The recipe for success: 'kneading' relations and quality together

Also in this latest evolution of Rana products, there is a glimpse of one of the elements of the recipe for success. These components move along two main guidelines that frequently intersect and nurture each other. The first is that of relations supporting and governing all strategic decisions of Pastificio Rana. These relations comprise all of the company, from the relations between Giovanni and Gianluca to those with all the employees and the clients of the firm. This guideline underlies all strategic and management decisions of Pastificio Rana.

The second is the decisive choice of product quality, which constantly evolves in both the substance of the products themselves and the production methods, thanks to innovation, constant yet gradual, which has typified Pastificio Rana from its very beginnings. This evolution has demonstrated relevant business acumen that has, on the one hand, contributed to the creation of a new productive sector and, on the other, has allowed Pastificio Rana undisputed leadership within it.

References

Álvarez, S. and Barney, J. (2004) 'Organising rent generation and appropriation: Toward a theory of the entrepreneurial firm', *Journal of Business Venturing* 19: 621–35.

Argenti, P. A. (2008) *Corporate Communication*, New York: McGraw-Hill.

Bisel R. S. (2010) 'A communicative ontology of organization? A description, history, and critique of CCO theories for organization science', *Management Communication Quarterly* 24(1): 124–31.

Burns, P. (2005) *Corporate entrepreneurship: building an entrepreneurial organisation*, Palgrave: Macmillan.

Busenitz, L. W., West, G. P., Shepherd, D., Nelson, T., Chandler, G. and Zacharakis, A. (2003) 'Entrepreneurship research in emergence', *Journal of Management* 29: 285–308.

Bygrave, W. D. (1989) 'The entrepreneurship paradigm (I): a philosophical look at its research methodologies', *Entrepreneurship: Theory and Practice* 14: 7–26.

Cooren, F., Taylor, J. R. and van Every, E. J. (2006) *Communication as organising*, Mahwah, NJ: Lawrence Erlbaum Associates.

Cornelissen, J. (2011) *Corporate Communication: A Guide to Theory and Practice*, London: Sage.

Daft, R. L. and Weick, K. E. (1984) 'Toward a model of organisations as interpretations systems', *Academy of Management Review* 9: 284–95.

Dew, N., Ramakrishna, V. S. and Venkataraman, S. (2004) 'Dispersed knowledge and an entrepreneurial theory of the firm', *Journal of Business Venturing* 19: 659–79.

Foss, N. J., Klein, P. G. (2005) 'Entrepreneurship and the economic theory of the firm: any gains from trade?', in Agarwal, R., Álvarez, S. A. and Sorenson, O. (eds) *Handbook of Entrepreneurship Research: Disciplinary Perspectives*, Dordrecht: Springer.

Invernizzi, E. and Romenti, S. (2009) 'Institutionalisation and Evaluation of Corporate Communication in Halian Companies', *International Journal of Strategic Communication* 3(2).

Invernizzi, E. and Romenti, S. (2013) 'Adopting an Entrepreneurial Perspective to the Study of Strategic Communication'. In D. Holtzhausen and A. Zerfass (eds) *Handbook of Strategic Communication*, Routledge.

Ireland, R. D., Hitt, M. A. and Sirmon, D. G. (2003) 'A model of strategic entrepreneurship: the construct and its dimensions', *Journal of Management* 29: 963–89.

Kuhn, T. A. (2008) 'Communicative theory of the firm: developing an alternative perspective on intra-organisational power and stakeholder relationships', *Organisation Studies* 29: 1227–54.

Meyer, J. W. and Rowan, B. (1977) 'Institutional organisations: formal structure as myth and ceremony', *American Journal of Sociology* 83: 340–63.

Putnam, L. L. and Nicotera, A. M. (2009) *Building theories of organisation: the constitutive role of communication*, New York: Routledge.

Reed, M. (2010) 'Is communication constitutive of organisation?', *Management Communication Quarterly* 24: 151–7.

Selznick, P. (1948) 'Foundations of the theory of organisation', *American Sociological Review* 13: 25–35.

Selznick, P. (1957) *Leadership in Administration*, New York, NY: Harper & Row.

Sewell, G. (2010) 'Metaphor, myth, and theory building: communication studies meets the linguistic turn in sociology, anthropology, and philosophy', *Management Communication Quarterly* 24: 139–50.

Teece, D. and Pisano, G. (1994) 'The dynamic capabilities of firms: an introduction', *Industrial and Corporate Change* 3(3): 537–56.

Teece, D. J., Pisano, G. and Shuen, A. (1997) 'Dynamic capabilities and strategic management', *Strategic Management Journal* 18: 509–33.

van Riel, C. B. M. (1995) *Principles of Corporate Communication*, London: Prentice Hall.

van Riel, C. and Fombrun, C. (2007) *Essentials of Corporate Communication*, New York: Routledge.

van Ruler, B. and Vercic, D. (2002) *The Bled Manifesto on Public Relations*, Ljubljana: Pristop.

Weick, K. E. (1995) *Sensemaking in organisations*, Thousand Oaks, CA: Sage Publications.

Zerfass, A. and Huck, S. (2007) 'Innovation, communication, and leadership: new developments in strategic communication', *International Journal of Strategic Communication* 1: 107–22.

7 Corporate branding
An employee perspective

Helen Stuart and
Belén Rodríguez-Cánovas

Introduction

A shown in Figure 7.1, corporate branding goes beyond product branding in that the corporate brand is based on the corporate identity, that is, the organisation's values, its promises, and its attitudes towards stakeholders and the environment. Corporate brands formerly emphasised two main stakeholders: customers and shareholders. However, employees are now being recognised for the crucial role they play in enacting the corporate brand. As Morsing and Kristensen (2001) write, organisational members are a significant attribute distinguishing corporate brands from product brands, since the values of a company become visible to many stakeholders through their interactions with organisational members, specifically employees. In other words, employees are a corporate brand resource (King and Grace 2008). Furthermore, employees (and potential employees) are stakeholders and, as such, are recipients of corporate brand messages as shown in Figure 7.2.

As Ind (2003) states, brands are about people, by which he meant that the attitudes and behaviours of employees have a major role in ensuring that the brand promise is successfully implemented. If employees enact the corporate brand they are said to 'live' the corporate brand (Ind 2001; Boyd and Sutherland 2006). An advertisement that was popular on Australian television demonstrated the extent to which employees are regarded as brand ambassadors.[1] The so-called 'barbecue test' advertisement begins with a bank employee at a barbecue being asked what he does for a living. When his reply is that he works for a bank the party action stops because in Australia banks generally have a poor image. The bank employee reassures everyone at the barbecue that he does not work for one of 'those' banks; rather he is employed by a more modern flexible bank (St George Bank). The partygoers breathe a collective sigh of relief and the party action resumes.

In this chapter, the issues that underpin the employee perspective on the corporate brand are discussed. Topics considered include: why employee identification with the corporate brand is important, what employee identification means in relation to organisational culture, the effect of organisational structure on employee identification, and how employee identification is impacted by corporate rebranding, a periodic strategy of the modern organisation.

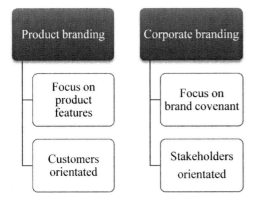

Figure 7.1 Product branding versus corporate branding

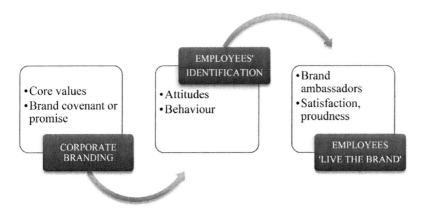

Figure 7.2 Employees as corporate brand resource

Employee identification and the corporate brand

The corporate brand can be thought of as a confirmation of the corporate identity, which is based on the organisational identity. The corporate brand represents a promise or covenant of what stakeholders can expect from the organisation in terms of their attitudes and behaviours. Therefore, employee identification is linked to the corporate brand in the sense that employee attitudes and behaviours influence, to a large extent, the way other stakeholders perceive whether or not the corporate brand lives up to its promise. As Ind (2001) pointed out some years ago, many employees don't actively support the corporate brand; one reason being that they don't know how to support it because they have not been engaged with the corporate brand in any meaningful way. The type and content of communication with employees is highlighted as is the need for managers to demonstrate clearly what is required of employees in terms of enacting the corporate brand.

Research into the link between organisational culture and brand success by de Chernatony and Cottam (2008) explored employee perceptions of organisational culture in relation to the brand. They found several 'cultural pitfalls' to avoid when on the quest for brand success. These included: inconsistency between the organisational culture and brand values, poorly thought out cultural changes, and too much focus on hard rather than soft organisational goals. All these affected the employees' ability to enact the corporate brand. The authors noted that a culture of fear and punishment negatively affects employees in that it is not conducive to them enacting the corporate brand to the best of their abilities (de Chernatony and Cottam 2008: 20). A discussion of organisation identity (on which the corporate identity and corporate brand are based) and employee identification is therefore a necessary part of understanding employees' conceptions of the corporate brand.

Employee identity and identification and organisational identity

Identification generally describes the extent to which individuals define themselves in terms of another individual or group (Pratt 1998). Brewer and Gardner (1996) classified identity as individual, relational and collective. In the case of employees, one or more of these identities may be operating in the work situation. For example, in the case of individual identity, an employee may perceive their job as a means to an end and retain a strong sense of their individualism. However, it is likely that relational identity operates as individuals relate to their co-workers. For example, in a factory, other workers may have an impact on how well an individual does their job and employees undertaking boring routine jobs often find the social interaction with other employees a source of job satisfaction. Collective identity exists when employees are actively engaged in the organisational culture, and where this occurs, the employee is potentially able to contribute to the attainment of the corporate brand promise.

Employee identification can be defined as the degree to which employees define themselves by the same attributes they believe define the organisation (Dutton *et al.* 1994: 239). How employees think of themselves in the organisation influences key outcomes at work, including effort, cooperation, organisational support, and citizenship behaviours (Bartel 2001; Dukerich *et al.* 2002; Mael and Ashforth 1992). In general, an employee is strongly identified with an organisation when his or her identity as an organisation member is more salient than alternative identities, and when his or her self-concept has many of the characteristics of the organisation as a social group. When individuals identify with their organisation, they pay attention to what they have in common with other organisational members (Brickson 2000). A good illustration of this identification has been provided by Garbett (1988: 2) who related the case of a 3M salesman who described himself as innovative and successful, projecting the 3M organisation.

Ashforth *et al.* (2008: 330) distinguish between organisational identity and organisational identification. Whereas organisational identity includes values, goals, beliefs and stereotypical traits – defined by Albert and Whetten (1985) as the central, distinctive and enduring attributes of the organisation – organisational identification involves individuals becoming prototypical of this identity in their thoughts (cognitive), feelings (affective) and actions (behavioural), which will only happen when the organisational identity is salient to them. For example, if the identity of an organisation involves values about caring for the environment, an employee who does not share these values may not feel or act in a way that signifies that their thoughts and feelings are aligned with the organisation, although they may still exhibit behavioural identification if there are rules and processes in place (such as rewards and punishments) which require such behaviour.

Morsing (2006) noted that companies are increasingly incorporating ethical and moral responsibilities in their corporate brand promise. Hence employees are now expected to commit to a moral imperative, whereas previously it was only an aesthetic commitment. This has the potential consequence of the corporate brand '(...) serving as a means of censorship on thinking and expression' (Morsing 2006:106). However, to some extent, employees choose to work for such organisations on the basis of already held values. A relevant concept is 'person-organisation fit (POF)' (O'Reilly and Chatman 1986; Stuart 2002; Yaniv and Farkas 2005). This concept deals with the congruence between an employee's personal values and the values of the organisation. Hence, a strong POF means a higher perceived congruence between organisational values and the individual values of the employee and also a high fulfilment of the corporate values by the employees. It is argued that the better this fit, the more employees will be committed to enacting the core values of the organisation. In this situation, the brand promise will be transferred to the customers 'as it is' and employees become ambassadors of the corporate values (Cable and DeRue 2002).

In yet another interpretation of employee identification, Rousseau (1998) maintained that the relevant literature demonstrates that the bases of corporate actions are cognitive processes in that individuals expand the way they think about themselves to include a larger sets of social objects (Parsons 1951; Etzioni 1961; Coleman 1990). 'Situated' identification is an elemental form of identification related to being part of a collective: this occurs when an individual perceives that his or her relationship to the organisation forms an 'us' (for example: a group working together to meet a deadline). This level of identification may be temporary and unstable because of its situational nature. At a deeper level, the 'deep structure', occurs when organisational identification becomes part of the employee's broader self-concept. This involves '(...) a congruence between self-at-work and one's broader self concept' (Rousseau 1998: 218).

There are implications in terms of employees and corporate rebranding from the above discussion of organisational identity and organisational identification. To begin with, Ashforth *et al.* (2008: 337), note some 'potentially negative implications of identification in organisations' which include 'resistance to organisational change'. Employees with affective and cognitive identification are more likely to experience negativity towards an organisational change (because of their deeper connection to the organisation) than those employees with only behavioural identification. The corporate rebranding process, discussed later in the chapter, often involves such an organisational change. However, Rousseau argued that deep structure identification can survive where organisational changes are perceived to have continuity with the past (Rousseau 1998: 227). By offering 'credible signals' an expanded zone of acceptance of the changes is possible. The importance of internal communication in the corporate rebranding process is discussed in a following section. The implication one can derive from Rousseau's analysis in terms of employee identification with the corporate brand is that 'deep structure' type employee identification with the present corporate brand is not necessarily antithetical to acceptance of a new rebranded corporate brand if there is a perception of continuity in the process. Further, the results of a study by van Knippenberg *et al.* (2006: 685) suggested that those employees who have deep structure identification with the organisation are more likely to be focused upon the change processes than on the change outcomes during organisational change. Therefore, when communicating a change in the corporate brand, employees with affective and cognitive identification will require persuasive communication about why the change was made so that they can enact the new corporate brand, whereas those with behavioural identification only will want information about how the new corporate brand will affect the way they are now expected to behave in their job.

In some organisations, affective identification is emphasised. In these types of organisations employees are recruited with the expectation that they will be emotionally involved with the core values. For example, companies like IKEA or Virgin explicitly refer to values and vision in their recruitment style to encourage affective employee identification. The Virgin website states that: 'Infusing our core values into everything we do relies on our company and our people doing their bit' (Virgin 2011). IKEA (2011) says, 'A key success factor has been the recruitment of committed individuals who have shared the IKEA vision and pulled together to turn it into a reality.' The way in which employees develop organisational identification is also dependent on the organisational structure as discussed next.

The effects of organisational structure on employee identification with the corporate brand

Mintzberg's organisational structure framework (1989) categorised organisations into different types, according to their structure. Using this framework, we can make some inferences about how organisational structure affects employees' ability to 'live' the corporate brand. Organisational structure impacts on the way in which employees identify with the organisation and hence the way in which they will relate to the corporate brand. Some organisational structures support employee identification from the 'heart', that is, affective identification (Ashforth *et al.* 2008), whereas for other structures identification will be with the 'head', that is, cognitive and/or behavioural identification (Ashforth *et al.* 2008), as explained below.

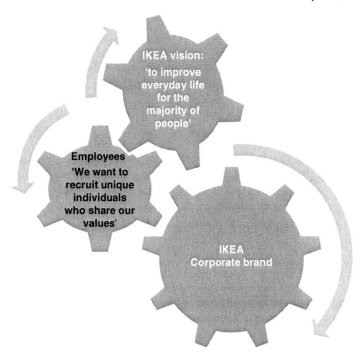

Figure 7.3 An example of an organisation where affective identification is emphasised

In missionary organisations the mission is more important than the people and in this type of organisation employees are expected to have deep structure identification with the mission, living the corporate brand with their 'heart' or affective identification. Employees in these types of organisations are expected to 'live' the corporate brand in a personal way; to be committed to a mission that has moral or ethical implications. Employees generally have to have some kind of prior commitments to the values inherent in the mission of such organisations. In this type of organisation, corporate rebranding is unlikely as the mission would have to change; if it did then a new organisation or organisational structure would be required.

Innovative structures are organisational structures that do not have any form of standardisation or coordination. These types of organisations operate in a dynamic environment which is unpredictable and hence favours an organic structure (Mintzberg 1989: 199, 207). The lack of standardisation in innovative organisations is a barrier to employee identification with a corporate brand. As the innovative process is central to the organisation, employees will identify with the process of innovation so employee identification is likely to be cognitive rather than affective. The corporate brand promise is based on the value of innovation.

Entrepreneurial organisational structures are simple structures, '(...) run firmly and personally by their leaders (...). They make for wonderful stories of the building of great empires and of dramatic turnarounds' (Mintzberg 1989: 116). In these types of organisations the leader has a personal vision for the success of the company. Therefore, employees will identify with their 'heart' – affective identification. Business systems are eventually developed so that the leader does not need to continue to articulate the vision personally but the employees will be expected to identify with the vision articulated when the organisation was formed. However, as the business expands beyond its entrepreneurial roots, the system developed may impose new expectations on the employees in terms of their behavioural identification.

Professional structures fall between 'head' and 'heart' in terms of employee identification. In these structures, proficiency is a major force, meaning that highly trained specialists operate in a relatively independent way with the emphasis on the work they do with their clients, patients and students. They are expected to work in a fairly standard way due to their professionalism and ethical standards. However, '(…) no matter how standardised the knowledge and skills, their complexity ensures that considerable discretion remains in their application. No two professionals – no two surgeons or engineers or social workers – ever apply them in exactly the same way' (Mintzberg 1989: 175). Because professionals are loyal to their profession, employee identification with the organisation is related to whether the organisation supports their professional principles. Professional employees are particularly sensitive to organisational changes that diminish personal responsibility and, therefore, corporate rebranding that promotes a more standardised approach to their work may decrease 'deep structure' employee identification and cause employees to move towards 'situated identification' (Rousseau 1998) unless there is a rationale for the change which the professionals accept.

An example of this issue of professional structures becoming more 'bureaucratised' can be found in an empirical study of the organisational identification of primary care physicians in a large non-profit health maintenance organisation (Herkman *et al.* 2009). Lower professional identification resulted in more organisational support whereas higher professional identification resulted in lower organisational support. Extrapolating these results to corporate branding, employees with higher levels of professional identification will be less likely to support a corporate rebranding process that involves less expected professionalism. An example can be found in universities as they become more corporatised and less focused on academic values and traditions.

The structures where 'head' or behavioural identification will be more important than 'heart' include machine structures where efficiency is the prime force. As Mintzberg (1989) stated, in these organisations '(…) we would also expect to find strong forces for the destruction of fledgling ideologies' (Mintzberg 1989: 234). Many government and semi-government agencies are machine in structure. Employees identify by the process of following systems and processes, that is, behavioural identification.

Diversified structures are based on the strategy of diversification and the synergy achieved by putting together a range of businesses, which then operate autonomously. Employee identification tends to be focused on their

Table 7.1 Organisational structure and employee identification

Type of organisational structure	Core belief or 'raison d'être'	Employee identification type in order of importance
Missionary	Mission	Affective and behavioural
Innovative	Innovation	Affective and behavioural
Entrepreneurial	Leader's vision	Cognitive and behavioural
Professional	Proficiency	Cognitive and affective with profession, behavioural with organisation
Machine	Efficiency	Behavioural
Diversified	Diversification	Affective and cognitive in the divisions, behavioural with organisation.

division – relational identity. If the organisation decides to rebrand to a monolithic corporate brand, then employees will still identify with their previous divisional brand because this is where they are focused in terms of business performance. Managing corporate rebranding in this type of structure is a balancing act; it may be essential to present a monolithic corporate brand to external audiences but employees in separate businesses will have primary identification with their division unless performance rewards are focused outside their division. So this may result in affective identification with their unit and behavioural identification with the company. Table 7.1 is a summary of this discussion of organisational structure and employee identification.

A critical issue for many companies is how to retain employee identification with the corporate brand and hence their enactment of the corporate brand to support a new or refocused brand covenant or promise. In the sections below we discuss the issues which affect employee identification in the case of a corporate rebranding.

The effects of corporate rebranding on employee identification

Rationale for the rebranding

The motivations for corporate rebranding include: mergers, acquisitions and divestitures, shifts in the marketplace caused by actions of competitors, changed economic or legal conditions, presenting a global image to the marketplace, and updating the corporate brand visual identity (Stuart and Muzellec 2004). Articulating the rationale to employees for the rebranding is an important component of whether or not it is readily enacted by those employees. The framework developed by Merrilees (2005) of brand vision, brand orientation, and brand strategy was shown in his case study of a Canadian tyre company to be effective; enabling employees to understand the rationale for the rebranding process.

As seen in the above discussion, the rationale for the rebranding is often not clearly understood or accepted by employees. Additionally, if the organisation is a service-oriented company, employees may be at the sharp end of customer dissatisfaction with the rebranding, listening to customer complaints, particularly when the rebranding has been responsible for an increase in costs to the consumer or a decrease in customer service levels.

Coherence of the corporate brand and rebrand

The corporate brand needs to be based on a 'coherent' identity for employees to live the brand (Balmer *et al.* 2009; Wheeler *et al.* 2006) and, as mentioned previously, this will be based on organisational culture which is '(...) embedded in its customs and rituals... [which]... endure longer than the corporate identity articulated by top managers' (Rodrigues and Child 2008: 890). Moreover, corporate identity definitions that were established early in the organisation's history are seen by employees '(...) as a point of reference against which the legitimacy of subsequent changes is evaluated' (Rodrigues and Child 2008: 890). Therefore, in a corporate rebranding process, decided upon by the managers of the organisation, the degree to which employees identify with the new corporate brand will depend upon the perceived degree of coherence, that is, logical consistency, with the present corporate brand and the underlying corporate identity.

Merrilees and Miller (2007: 540) predicted that the most successful corporate rebrands were evolutionary rather than revolutionary. They argued that: 'Successful corporate rebranding may require retaining at least some core or peripheral brand concepts to build a bridge from the existing corporate brand to the revised corporate brand.' A complete change, such as happened at British Airways when they became an international rather than a British airline, was perceived negatively by employees, who were committed to the British way of doing things as reflected in the corporate brand (Balmer *et al.* 2009).

The management of coherency in corporate branding is complicated (Morsing and Kristensen (2001) as different stakeholders hold different views of the corporate brand. In a case study by Morsing and Kristensen (2001), coherence was examined from two perspectives: coherence over time and across stakeholders. The researchers found that the employees and a group of external stakeholders, specifically the media, held different views about the corporate brand, that is, 'statement coherency', defined as the coherency with which the management expressed the corporate brand covenant by consistent communication. However, the employees and external stakeholders shared a general understanding about the uniqueness of the organisation in question which the authors referred to as 'uniqueness coherency'. In other words, although the two groups did not share an exactly similar understanding of the corporate brand, their interpretations were similar enough. However, the authors noted a danger in allowing very different interpretations to gain momentum. This will be a continuing issue for corporate brand managers, particularly in corporate rebranding situations.

The importance of narratives in organisational change is highlighted in a study by Berendse *et al.* (2006). To make sense of a new situation, organisational actors '(…) try to align their perception of the new situation with their view of the old situation, thereby creating a narrative account of what is going on from their perspective'. The process of change is therefore perceived by employees as '(…) a struggle over the acceptance, adoption and dissemination of alternate change narratives in order to legitimize or delegitimize the process of change' (Berendse *et al.* 2006: 80). The implication from this study is that the more employees are exposed to a coherent narrative about the change, the more they will identify with the new corporate brand as they will perceive it as a legitimate narrative.

A case in point is the radical revitalisation of two famous brands, Nike and Starbucks (Bedbury 2002). Ironically, each of these brands had gone through a period where the brand owners simply relied on hope or intuition that other stakeholders would comprehend the brand essence meaning. The development of the 'Just Do It' campaign was associated with greater definition in Nike's brand mantra towards 'Authentic, Athletic, Performance'. Similarly the initial fuzzy Starbucks brand identity was transformed into 'Rewarding Everyday Moments'. In both cases Bedbury used unorthodox market research, including issues-based research and monitoring for Nike and a 500-year history of coffee houses for Starbucks. The subsequent greater clarity of the brand mantra (vision) facilitated the brand alignment inside each corporation (Bedbury 2002).

Degree of rebranding

While some rebranding occurs at an incremental level, for example, an update of the corporate logo, some rebranding programmes are at the other extreme where the name, slogan and logo are changed (Stuart and Muzellec 2004). Brand revitalisation is the process by which companies keep their brands fresh and relevant to the market (Merrilees 2005; Muzellec and Lambkin 2006). Small changes in the logo may be well accepted by employees whereas changes in the logo, slogan and name at the same time, referred to by Merrilees (2005) and Muzellec and Lambkin (2006) as brand revolution, take more time and consideration to implement and are more relevant to a discussion of employee identification.

Certain organisational types, such as diversified structures, will be more likely to implement a total rebranding of name, slogan and logo. Changes in the direction of this type of organisation will require businesses which previously had their own corporate brands to become part of the over-arching monolithic brand. The process of branding and rebranding in diversified structures is largely based on external factors such as becoming a globally focused company, responding to market conditions in a particular country and as a result of mergers and acquisitions. Employees in the process may experience negative feelings towards the new corporate brand and wonder at its relevance to them as they continue doing the same job in the same office in the same location as before the rebranding.

A change in the slogan and logo without any apparent rationale can be viewed by employees as a wasteful exercise. Here there may be an 'emphasis on labels, not meanings', referred to by Gotsi and Andriopoulos (2007: 346) as a pitfall of the corporate rebranding process. It sometimes happens that livery, including signage, stationery and uniforms, are changed while employees are being asked to accept wage or salary cuts or other budget savings for example. Rebranding the logo when nothing has changed in terms of the expectations of employees performing their jobs is viewed negatively, as was found in an empirical study of an Australian supermarket brand. As well, employees believed that the new brand was costly since it did not improve profitability (Bues and Matanda 2010).

Employees' identification with an organisation has been shown to be based on what they believe the organisation is about, that is, what is distinctive, central, and enduring about it (Albert and Whetten 1985), and also what employees believe that outsiders think about the organisation (Dutton *et al.* 1994). In the case of the supermarket study by Bues and Matanda (2010), employees articulated that customers were still calling the brand by its previous name, so there was no reason for them to support the rebranding. Muzellec and Lambkin (2006) also noted that their case studies of corporate rebranding highlighted that: '(…) the role of employees is equally crucial in determining customers' feelings towards the brand', since their experiences of the brand will be as a result of interactions with employees.

Internal communication

How much and what to communicate to employees about the new corporate brand is one which is often left until issues that impact on the communications during and after the rebranding process have been discussed. Organisations vary in the extent and quality of communication to employees regarding corporate rebranding. For example, when Vodafone acquired Eircell, the internal communication was well managed according to researchers Daly and Moloney (2004). However, in the case of the Australian supermarket brand, there was no integrated communication strategy; some employees were told of the changes in store meetings while others received a memo in their payslips (Bues and Matanda 2010). While it would seem logical that employees are more likely to support the new corporate brand when clear formal communication of the new corporate brand is undertaken and continued during the rebranding process, what is being communicated is equally important. In research in which organisational identification was measured before and after a merger, trust in the merger was a significant predictor of organisational commitment by employees after the merger (Bartels *et al.* 2006). The implication can be made that what is being communicated about a corporate rebrand is not as important as whether it is credible to employees. Also, communication needs to be developed as the rebranding process proceeds. In their study of a merger, Bartels *et al.* (2006) found that employee satisfaction with the amount and quality of the communication of information prior to the merger improved their expected post-merger identification.

The type of employee identification, discussed previously, is also an important factor. Those employees with deep structure identification will value communication relating to the process of rebranding including the rationale and the connection with the previous corporate brand – the 'whys' – whereas those employees with lower levels of identification will require communication related to the outcomes of the rebranding process such as potential and actual changes in their work processes, salaries, job designs and the like.

The effect of the issues on enactment of the new corporate brand

As mentioned previously, some organisational structures tend to promote employee identification that is affective and/or behavioural whereas other structures encourage employee identification that is primarily behavioural. Therefore, enactment of the new corporate rebrand by employees will vary accordingly.

In enacting the new corporate brand, leadership will be an important part of the process. By answering the implicit question 'Who are we now?' organisational leaders communicate with employees about the new corporate brand and how the brand promise can be enacted. They will lead by enacting the new brand in their emotions, thinking and behaviour. Therefore, leaders should agree about and reflect the types of activities that make the new corporate brand distinctive (Voss *et al.* 2006: 753). Employees whose identification is primarily through the processes associated with the new corporate brand, such as strategies for becoming

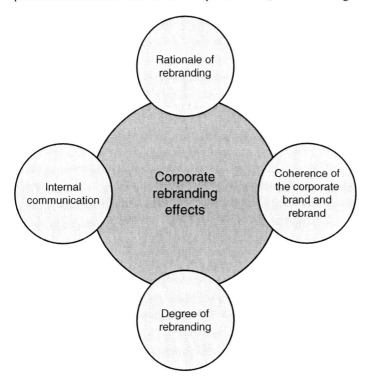

Figure 7.4 Effects of corporate rebranding on employee identification

more customer-focused, will enact the new corporate brand in accordance with how well the organisation changes its processes to reflect the new corporate brand covenant.

The attractiveness of the corporate brand to external stakeholders also impacts on employee enactment of the new corporate brand. Employees '(…) keep one eye on the organisational mirror' (Dutton and Dukerich 1991: 551) when they enact the new corporate brand. Therefore, as well as employees reflecting the new corporate brand in their interactions with external stakeholders, these stakehold-ers will also provide feedback to employees on their approval or disapproval with the new corporate brand promise. This feedback needs to be taken account of and reflected upon by organisational managers.

Vital questions in relation to employee enactment of the corporate brand

The discussion in this chapter has been about the issues and challenges employees face when trying to enact the corporate brand and be effective brand ambassa-dors. Unfortunately, many companies assume that once they have decided on a corporate brand or corporate rebrand, employees will 'get on board' and play their role in the success of the corporate brand by 'living' the corporate brand. In this chapter it has been demonstrated that taking a generic approach to the process of using employees to convert the corporate brand promise into a reality for other stakeholders is a mistake. Particular organisations face particular sets of chal-lenges in relation to employees attempting to enact the corporate brand. Some vital questions for organisational managers are:

- What is the current level of employee engagement with the corporate brand? Why is this so?
- What levels of identification (affective, cognitive and behavioural) exist in relation to organisational identity? Are there groups of employees that exhibit prototypical identification? Is the identification mainly 'situated' or 'deep structure'? What are the characteristics of each group?
- What type of organisational structure is characteristic of your organisation and how have you considered how this affects employee identification and hence enactment of the corporate brand?
- To what extent are the organisational culture and corporate brand aligned? Is there a need for greater alignment?
- How are expectations of enacting the corporate brand communicated to employ-ees, given the level of their identification with the organisational identity?
- How are employees included in the process of corporate rebranding?

Conclusion

The focus in this chapter has been the employee in relation to the enactment of the corporate brand. The main conclusion that can be drawn from this analysis is that careful consideration of the way an organisation's employees think, feel and act towards the corporate brand is an essential part of the process of corporate brand success. The interactions between organisational culture, corporate identity and organisational structure are key antecedents in employee identification with the corporate brand.

As well as considering these factors in corporate branding, further considerations when expecting employees to 'live' a new corporate brand after rebranding include communicating the rationale for the change with signals that have the potential to be positively interpreted by employees.

Note

1 St George Bank advertisement: Youtube, available at: http://www.youtube.com/watch?v=YL3XdEqKUOs

References

Albert, S. and Whetten, D. (1985) 'Organisational identity', in Cummings, L. L. and Staw, B. M. (eds) *Research in organisational behavior*, Greenwich CT: JAI Press, 263–95.

Ashforth, B., Harrison, S. and Corley, K. (2008) 'Identification in organisations: An examination of four fundamental questions', *Journal of Management* June: 325–74.

Balmer, J. M. T., Stuart, H. and Greyser, S. (2009) 'Corporate identity and corporate brand alignment: the strategic positioning of British Airways in the 20th century', *California Management Review* 51(3): 6–23.

Bartel, C. A. (2001) 'Social comparisons in boundary-spanning work: effects of community outreach on members' organisational identity and identification', *Administrative Science Quarterly* 46: 379–413.

Bartels, J., Douwes, R., de Jong, M. and Pruyn, A. (2006) 'Organisational identification during a merger: Determinants of employees' expected identification with the new organisation', *British Journal of Management* 17: 49–67.

Bedbury, S. (2002) *A New Brand World: Principles for Achieving Brand Leadership in the 21st Century*, New York: Viking.

Berendse, M., Duijnhoven, H. and Veenswijk, V. (2006) 'Editing narratives of change. Identity and legitimacy in complex innovative infrastructure organisations', *Intervention Research* 2: 73–89.

Boyd, G. and Sutherland, M. (2006) 'Obtaining employee commitment to living the brand of the organisation', *South African Journal of Business Management* 37(1): 9–20.

Brewer, M. B. and Gardner, W. (1996) 'Who is this "we"? Levels of collective identity and self representations', *Journal of Personality and Social Psychology* 71: 83–93.

Brickson, S. (2000) 'The impact of identity orientation on individual and organisational outcomes in demographically diverse settings', *Academy of Management Review* 25: 82–101.

Bues, S. and Matanda, M. (2010) 'Employees' perceptions of rebranding process: Case study of rebranding of an Australian supermarket chain', proceedings of the Australian and New Zealand Marketing Academy Conference, Christchurch, NZ.

Cable, D. M. and DeRue, D. S. (2002) 'The congruent and discriminant validity of subjective fit perceptions', *Journal of Applied Psychology* 87(5): 875–84.

Coleman, J. (1990) *Foundations of Social Theory*, Cambridge, MA: Belknap Press.

Cooper, D. and Thatcher, S. (2010) 'Identification in organisations: The role of self-concept orientations and identification motivations', *Academy of Management Review* 35(4): 516–38.

Daly, A. and Moloney, D. (2004) 'Managing corporate rebranding', *Irish Marketing Review* 17(2): 30–36.

de Chernatony, L. and Cottam, S. (2008) 'Interactions between organisational cultures', *Journal of Brand Management* 17(1): 13–24.

Dukerich, J. M., Golden, B. R. and Shortell, S. M. (2002) 'Beauty is in the eye of the beholder: The impact of organisational identification, identity, and image on the cooperative behaviors of physicians', *Administrative Science Quarterly* 47: 507–33.

Dutton, J. and Dukerich, J. (1991) 'Keeping an eye on the mirror: Image and identity in organisational adaptation', *Academy of Management Journal* 34(3): 517–54.

Dutton, J., Dukerich, J. and Harquail, C. (1994) 'Organisational images and member identification', *Administrative Science Quarterly* 39: 239–63.

Edwards, M. (2005) 'Organisational identification: A conceptual and operational review', *International Journal of Management Reviews* 7(4): 207–30.

Etzioni, A. (1961) *A Comparative Analysis of Complex Organisations*, New York: Free Press.

Garbett, Th. (1988) *How to Build a Corporation's Identity and Project Its Image*, Lexington, MA: D. C. Heath.

Gotsi, M. and Andriopoulos, C. (2007) 'Understanding the pitfalls of the corporate rebranding process', *Corporate Communications: An International Journal* 12(4): 341–55.

—— (2008) 'Corporate re-branding: is cultural alignment the weakest link?', *Management Decision* 46(1): 46–57.

Herkman, D., Bigley, G., Steensma, H. and Hereford, J. (2009) 'Combined effects of organisational and professional identification on the reciprocity dynamic for professional employees', *Academy of Management Journal* 52(3): 506–26.

IKEA website (2011) 'It takes a dream to create a successful business idea. It takes people to make dreams a reality. Could you be one of those people?', online, available at: http://www.ikea.com/ms/en_US/jobs/join_us/index.html (accessed 1 June 2011).

Ind, N. (2001) *Living the Brand: How to Transform Every Member of Your Organisation into a Brand Champion*, United Kingdom: Kogan Page Ltd.

—— (2003) 'Inside out: How employees build value', *Journal of Brand Management* 10(6): 393–402.

Kennedy, S. H. (1977) 'Nurturing corporate images: total communication or ego trip?', *European Journal of Marketing* 11(3): 120–64.

King, C. and Grace, D. (2008) 'Internal branding: Exploring the employee's perspective', *Journal of Brand Management* 15(5): 358–72.

Mael, F. and Ashforth, B. E. (1992) 'Alumni and their alma mater: A partial test of the reformulated model of organizational identification', *Journal of Organizational Behavior* 13: 103–23.

Mael, F. and Ashforth, B. (2001) 'Identification in work, war, sports, and religion: Contrasting the benefits and risks', *Journal for the Theory of Social Behaviour* 31(2): 197–222.

Maxwell, R. and Knox, S. (2009) 'Motivating employees to "live the brand": a comparative case study of employer brand attractiveness within the firm', *Journal of Marketing Management* 25(9–10): 893–907.

Merrilees, B. (2005) 'Radical brand evolution: A case-based framework', *Journal of Advertising Research* June: 201–10.

Merrilees, B. and Miller, D. (2007) 'Principles of corporate rebranding', *European Journal of Marketing* 42(5–6): 537–52.

Mintzberg, H. (1989) *Mintzberg on Management*, United States: The Free Press.

Morsing, M. (2006) 'Corporate moral branding: limits to aligning employees', *Corporate Communications: An International Journal* 11(2): 97–108.

Morsing, M. and Kristensen, J. (2001) 'The question of coherency in corporate branding – over time and across stakeholders', *Journal of Communication Management* 6(1): 24–40.

Muzellec, L. and Lambkin, M. (2006) 'Corporate rebranding: destroying, transferring or creating brand equity', *European Journal of Marketing* 40(7–8): 803–24.

O'Reilly, C. and Chatman, J. (1986) 'Organisational commitment and psychological commitment: the effect of compliance, identification and internalisation on prosocial behaviour', *Journal of Applied Psychology* 71: 492–9.

Parsons, T. (1951) *The Social System*, Glencoe, IL: Free Press.

Pratt, M. G. (1998) 'To be or not to be? Central questions in organisational identification', in Whetten, D. and Godfrey, P. (eds) (1998) *Identity in Organisations: Building Theory Through Conversations*, Thousand Oaks, CA: Sage, 171–207.

Rodrigues, S. and Child, J. (2008) 'The development of corporate identity: A political perspective', *Journal of Management Studies* 45(5): 885–911.

Rousseau, D. M. (1998) 'Why workers still identify with organisations', *Journal of Organisational Behavior* 19: 217–33.

Stuart, H. (2002) 'Employee Identification with the Corporate Identity: Issues and Implications', *International Studies of Management and Organisation* 32(3): 29–45.

Stuart, H. and Muzellec, L. (2004) 'Corporate makeovers: can a hyena be rebranded?', *Journal of Brand Management* 11(6): 472–82.

van Knippenberg, B., Martin, L. and Tyler, T. (2006) 'Process-orientation versus outcome orientation during organisational change: The role of organisational identification', *Journal of Organisational Behavior* 27: 685–704.

Virgin website (2011) 'Culture and values', online, available at: http://www.virginaustralia.com/AboutUs/Careers/Cultureandvalues/index.htm (accessed 1 June 2011).

Voss, Z., Cable, D. M. and Voss, G. B. (2006) 'Organisational identity and firm performance: What happens when leaders disagree about "who we are"?', *Organisation Science* 16(6): 741–55.

Wheeler, A. R., Richey, R. G., Tokkman, M. and Sablynski, C. J. (2006) 'Retaining employees for service competency: The role of corporate brand identity', *Journal of Brand Management* 14(1–2): 96–113.

Yaniv, E. and Ferenc Farkas, F. (2005) 'The impact of person–organisation fit on the corporate brand perception of employees and of customers', *Journal of Change Management* 5(4): 447–61.

Part 3
Brand, CSR and reputation

8 Successfully establishing a green image for an established detergent brand

The 'Small and Mighty' case

Johan van Rekom and Gabriela Sinai

Introduction

Currently, being 'green' is great. We see companies massively engaging in communicating how green they are. Emphasising the reduction in carbon footprint of a company's activities can be fruitful. Wal-Mart replaced its fluorescent lights with 70 per cent more energy-efficient LED lights, leading to a significant reduction of its carbon footprint. This way, the company at the same time reduced its costs and served a social objective (Karnani 2011). However, not all observers may be equally convinced about the company's environmental consciousness, and the risk of suspicion of greenwashing may withhold managers from claiming environmental consciousness when the company has no history of doing so. Warnings against and wariness of window-dressing and greenwashing abound (Walker and Wan 2012), and managers are well advised to use communication about an organisation's environmental prowess carefully, so as not to come across as insincere or inauthentic and not to compromise the brand's credibility (Balmer 2012; Vallaster *et al.* 2012). How, now, would credibly becoming environmentally conscious be feasible under such circumstances?

The focal brand of our case study, Omo, is a detergent brand with a substantial market share in the Netherlands. Slightly over five years ago it brought to the market a much more concentrated version, which needed less packaging material, less water for every machine washing, and because of its smaller size, less cardboard for bulk packaging and less truck space for transportation, leading to a considerable reduction of the brand's carbon footprint. The manufacturers called this new variation of their brand 'Small and Mighty'. The development of concentrated detergents was quite successful, and internationally welcomed by retailer chains that wanted to develop a green policy such as Wal-Mart (Lai *et al.* 2010). This caused competitors to develop small concentrated versions of their detergents as well, opening perspectives to a considerable reduction of water consumption and carbon footprint. This way, the development of a concentrated package was more than just talk, but an action that had impact beyond the scope of the brand itself. Given its impact, the development of the concentrated version of Omo could thus be classified as a 'strong CSR performance' that positively reflects on the firm (Parguel *et al.* 2011). However, how would the brand come across to the average consumer, who lacks this kind of business information?

Along with many other brands, Omo did not have a clear 'green' previous history as such. Therefore, the risk might be real for some suspicion from the side of customers that green profiling may be about taking advantage of a fashionable concern rather than from sincere environmental consciousness. This risk is the more serious as green claims have surged in these recent years of worries about the environment, climate and global warming. They have become an important ingredient for brands to show their social responsibility, which is important to appeal not only to groups of consumers, but also to investors: fund managers are becoming more and more sensitive to material risks associated with sustainability issues (Chouinard *et al.* 2011). It has become appealing for brands to highlight what is 'green' about them and make this 'greenness' an important part of their positioning strategy (Delmas and Cuerel Burbano 2011; Parguel *et al.* 2011).

The huge production of green claims by diverse brands and industries brings about scepticism among consumers (Delmas and Cuerel Burbano 2011), putting stakeholders' perception of the company's ethical identity at stake (Balmer *et al.* 2007). Customers have become increasingly cynical and suspicious (Forehand and Grier 2003; Vlachos *et al.* 2009). Scepticism diminishes the effectiveness of such claims (Pomering and Johnson 2009), and could in the end even lead to adverse effects, as consumers may no longer believe the company is authentic in its behaviour, because it is engaging in contrived messages with the intent to serve economic purposes. They may see commercial goals behind it, either directly favouring enhanced sales, or image promotional motives.

If an organisation is under suspicion of pretending to help society or specific customers while its nice words just hide desires for growth and profit, it risks coming across as fake rather than as real, and its efforts will appear artificially tailored to customers' dreams and desires rather than a natural outgrowth of what the organisation is, casting doubt on the authenticity of the green claims. Such doubts, in the end, may seriously backfire on the brand (Balmer *et al.* 2007).

This creates an important dilemma for the positioning of brands like Omo. On the one hand issues of sustainability and the carbon footprint need to be addressed, and it seems worthwhile to communicate about the organisation's efforts in this area. Therefore, 'Green Marketing' can be considered an area whose importance may still substantially increase in future (Bears *et al.* 2009; Schlegelmilch and Öbersieder 2010). On the other hand, we live in a world where green claims are increasingly mistrusted. It is crucial for brand managers to know how they can get out of this dilemma when designing a green positioning for their brands. The key question this case study addresses, therefore, is: 'Can a green positioning of a brand without green history occur in such a way that consumers will indeed appreciate it as environmentally conscious?'

Challenge: safeguarding the authenticity of the greener brand

As we argued above, the purity of the perceived motives behind the green claims is a key issue. Beverland and Farrelly (2010) found this purity of motive to be one of the cornerstones of how consumers define authenticity. In the end, staying true to one's morals is a sign of virtuousness. Virtuousness is important for creating a favourable customer attitude towards the brand. Perceptions of virtuousness convey desirable consumer meanings of lack of pretention and genuine commitment to their claims (Thompson *et al.* 2006: 53). Clients have an inclination to peel away brand veneer, looking for the 'local merchant, as a stalwart citizen of the community' (Holt 2002: 88). If customers perceive genuine interest to be the driver of the organisation's societal endeavours, this is likely to reflect positively on their intentions to remain loyal to the organisation (Vlachos *et al.* 2009). If this genuine interest appears to be lacking, problems arise for a brand. After Starbucks' enormous growth some stakeholders wondered as to whether its emotional branding veiled expansionist motives which included strategies such as crushing local competition in order to reap high profits — suspicions which made its emotional branding promises come across as inauthentic. The perceived loss of authenticity of Starbucks threatened to erode its customer base (Thompson *et al.* 2006). Consumers are thus likely to associate authenticity with a brand's environmental engagement being driven by genuine environmental consciousness.

A brand's genuine care for the environment provides an alternative explanation for the potential default assumption that a brand engages in green marketing for commercial reasons. Whenever brands make claims that could risk coming across as inauthentic and inducing scepticism, people may wish to verify such claims (Beverland and Farrelly 2010). Therefore, this potential default assumption is likely to be weakened if clients believe that an organisation's environmental consciousness is a plausible explanation for what they observe. However, the average consumer is unlikely to have accurate information about the motives of brands and their manufacturing organisations. In the absence of such information, people will have to rely on what they believe to be relevant of what they know about the brand. If consumers' knowledge about product and brand features is limited, impressions about a brand's personality are likely to come to the fore. In what way do consumers' hunches about a brand's personality help them in assessing the authenticity of green brand claims?

The key to answering this question might be in the way the green claims are related to the consumers' hunches of the brand's personality and help them explain why the brand is what it is. People have a tendency to strongly rely on causal explanations in making sense of the world around them (Keil 2006). Brand personality features may play an important role in helping consumers understand why a brand might care about the environment. A brand's claim can be said to reflect what the brand is either if it is an established characteristic of the brand, or if it logically flows forth from characteristics consumers associate with a brand. For instance, if a brand is perceived as a warm, caring personality a green claim is much more plausible and easy to explain than if the brand is perceived to be rugged and harsh. Consumers may perceive a claim like environmental consciousness to derive from other features of a brand. In that case they will be less suspicious of commercial intentions underlying the brand's green profile and perceive the green claim to be more authentic.

The important issue to be investigated, thus, is whether Omo's possible environmental consciousness, as suggested by its green claims, relates to the personality features with which consumers would tend to describe the brand. If consumers see this environmental consciousness as related to other features of the brand, we may interpret this as a sign of acceptance of the green claims, whereas if a brand's alleged 'environmental consciousness' remains isolated and is unable to explain or to be explained by anything, green claims are likely to be unsuccessful.

Teasing out how consumers describe Omo

The personality features that might be relevant for the positioning of Omo have been collected in two small qualitative studies held before the introduction of the 'small and mighty' version of the brand. Twelve short open-ended interviews served for establishing those traits that applied to the version of the brand before the introduction of 'small and mighty'. Consumers were asked to picture Omo as a human being, and to tell what kind of human being Omo would be. The features mentioned by at least half of them served as an input into the questionnaire used in this research project. These were: 'reliable', 'caring', 'friendly', 'committed', 'helpful', 'down to earth', and 'honest'. To select features that might characterise consumers' ideal of Omo, 16 other consumers were asked what personality features they would like to see in a detergent brand. These latter interviews revealed five features that were desirable to at least half of those consumers: 'original', 'modern', 'joyful', 'lively' and 'expressive' (see Table 8.1). We supplemented these with 'environmental consciousness' as the 13th characteristic – the focal characteristic for this case study.

The key information needed is the degree to which this alleged 'environmental consciousness' is perceived to be related to the personality characteristics of the brand. Therefore, for each of the 12 other features, the causal relations were established as follows. For example, the relationship between the brand's characteristic of helpfulness and its environmental consciousness was proposed as: 'Omo is environmentally conscious, because Omo is helpful.' If respondents believed that Omo indeed was environmentally conscious because of its helpfulness, this was coded as '1'; if they believed that there was no relation at all or if the relation made sense but did not apply to Omo this was coded as '0'; and if they believed that Omo's helpfulness impeded its environmental consciousness this was coded as '−1'. These questions regarding causal relations were also asked for all possible combinations of the total 13 characteristics (including 'environmental consciousness') because this allowed us to check to what extent the features that would cause most other features were also perceived as Omo's most essential features (van Rekom *et al.* 2009). Perceived authenticity of each

Table 8.1 Respondents' ratings of the characteristics of Omo

	Applies to Omo		I like this about Omo		Without this feature Omo is no longer Omo		Causal status of this feature		Perceived feature authenticity	
	Mean	s.d.	Mean	s.d.	Mean	s.d.	Mean	s.d.	Mean	s.d.
Reliable	4.70	1.27	5.12	1.47	5.00	2.06	4.44	3.78	5.50	1.09
Caring	4.13	1.24	4.15	1.44	4.28	1.74	3.35	3.35	5.05	1.39
Friendly	4.32	1.18	4.54	1.27	4.17	1.51	2.81	3.29	4.75	1.30
Committed	3.87	1.35	4.44	1.43	4.28	1.49	3.81	4.04	5.00	1.24
Helpful	4.13	1.33	4.44	1.34	4.67	1.65	3.63	2.92	5.24	1.27
Down to earth	4.23	1.35	3.98	1.19	3.72	1.67	2.12	3.18	4.17	1.43
Honest	4.47	1.27	4.85	1.35	4.83	1.47	3.75	3.70	4.84	1.32
Joyful	4.28	1.42	4.29	1.42	3.78	1.40	0.76	2.17	4.02	1.36
Lively	4.17	1.45	4.27	1.52	3.78	1.31	1.12	1.54	3.98	1.33
Original	3.64	1.37	4.29	1.54	3.61	1.72	0.38	1.82	3.56	1.12
Modern	3.60	1.48	3.95	1.41	3.17	1.95	0.56	4.57	3.47	1.37
Expressive	3.55	1.10	3.88	1.31	3.61	1.38	0.53	1.55	3.30	1.19
Environmentally conscious	3.96	1.35	4.76	1.39	4.17	1.79	3.81	3.95	4.62	1.44

of the features was measured with three seven-point semantic differential scales (fake–real, inauthentic–authentic and artificial–natural). Three seven-point scales from Kent and Allen (1994) (familiar/unfamiliar, inexperienced/experienced and not knowledgeable/knowledgeable) served to control for respondents' familiarity with Omo. Respondents were asked to indicate on a seven-point scale the extent to which they liked each of the features of Omo.

These questions were part of a larger survey about the current position of Omo, which produced a relatively long questionnaire. Given the length of the questionnaire, a snowball sample relying on the network of the second author was believed to be adequate. Respondents were asked to reserve 25 minutes of their time to fill in the online questionnaire. Because, according to a recent nationwide survey, doing the washing was still a task taken care of nearly exclusively by women (Breedveld *et al.* 2006), the link to the electronic questionnaire was sent to women only. In a period of one month, 52 people had started filling in the questionnaire. Alas, the length of the questionnaire proved relatively problematic, leading to a small group of 15 women who had filled in the questionnaire completely, on average 31.5 years old, with a standard deviation of 10.0 years. For the composite scales we computed the averages of the items constituting them.

The reliabilities of the relevant measures were satisfactory to good: for perceived authenticity of Omo's green claims (M= 4.62, s.d. = 1.44), Cronbach alpha was 0.92. For familiarity with Omo (M = 4.01, s.d. = 1.49), Cronbach alpha was 0.82. In exploratory factor analyses, each of these multiple-item scales loaded on one single factor. Table 8.1 shows for all personality characteristics as well as for environmental consciousness the degree to which respondents believed it to apply to Omo, the degree they liked that feature of Omo, the degree to which they believed that Omo would no longer be Omo without that feature.

Table 8.2 shows the net proportions of agreement among respondents with the existence of causal relations between each of the features. For instance, Table 8.2 shows the number of 0.42 for the relation 'Omo is caring because Omo is reliable'. This number is arrived at as follows: of the 33 respondents, 15 agreed (coded as 1, see above), so gross agreement would be 15/33 = 0.45. One person disagreed (expressed as a proportion: 0.03). The proportion of disagreements is subtracted from the proportion of agreements, which leads to a net agreement of 0.45 − 0.03 = 0.42. This way, all numbers were calculated. Figure 8.1 gives a visual summary of this network of causal explanations, showing all relations with a net proportion of agreement higher than 0.35.

Ahn (1998) found that the extent to which people believe features to cause other features – in her terms, the feature's 'causal status' – predicts the extent to which a feature is deemed to be essential, i.e. the extent to which Omo would no longer be Omo without this feature. A higher causal status is thus an indication that the respective feature is part of the core of the brand. Table 8.1 lists both the causal status of each feature as well as the extent to which each feature is essential. It shows that 'reliable' is the feature that is most essential, and likewise the feature that has the highest causal status. The causal status of 'environmentally conscious' is 3.81 (Table 8.1), implying that in the eyes of our respondents, Omo's environmental consciousness on average caused 3.81 other features of this brand. Interestingly, the causal status of 'environmentally conscious' in Table 8.1 is second highest, after 'reliable' (4.44), and at par with 'committed' (3.81). This suggests that environmental consciousness is well embedded within the overall network of causal explanations of the features of Omo – an impression that is confirmed by the relatively high number of agreed-upon relations in Table 8.2 and the position of 'environmentally conscious' in Figure 8.1.

Figure 8.1 shows this embedment of 'environmental consciousness' in how consumers think about Omo – in particular as an explanation for Omo's personality traits. However, to what extent does a larger causal role for environmental consciousness imply that Omo's environmental consciousness comes across as more authentic? A regression analysis with perceived authenticity of Omo's environmental consciousness as the dependent variable and the causal status of environmental consciousness as the independent variable indeed shows a significant positive regression coefficient (β = 0.20, s.e. = 0.07, p = 0.01, R^2 = 0.37). Apparently, for the question as to whether claimed environmental consciousness is perceived to be authentic it is important that environmental consciousness is the source explaining Omo's personality features. Interestingly, the extent to

Table 8.2 Net agreement on the relations between Omo's features

Omo is: Because it is:	Reliable	Caring	Friendly	Committed	Helpful	Down to earth	Honest	Joyful	Lively	Original	Modern	Expressive	Environmentally conscious
Reliable	—	0.42	0.38	0.36	0.39	0.22	0.58	0.21	0.06	0.19	0.30	0.16	0.35
Caring	0.52	—	0.27	0.50	0.32	0.22	0.42	0.21	0.06	0.10	0.13	0.05	0.39
Friendly	0.38	0.21	—	0.27	0.18	0.16	0.32	0.50	0.17	0.00	0.08	0.21	0.17
Committed	0.48	0.45	0.35	—	0.29	0.16	0.53	0.21	0.18	0.10	0.17	0.16	0.30
Helpful	0.62	0.41	0.27	0.59	—	0.16	0.33	0.26	0.06	0.14	0.13	0.16	0.22
Down to earth	0.43	0.09	0.00	0.09	0.07	—	0.53	0.11	0.06	0.05	0.04	0.00	0.22
Honest	0.52	0.30	0.38	0.41	0.32	0.25	—	0.21	0.06	0.19	0.17	0.11	0.35
Joyful	-0.05	-0.03	0.23	0.09	0.11	-0.06	0.05	—	0.28	0.10	0.04	0.16	0.00
Lively	-0.05	-0.06	0.15	0.09	0.07	-0.03	0.11	0.47	—	0.05	0.08	0.21	0.00
Original	0.00	0.00	0.12	0.00	0.00	0.03	0.05	0.16	0.06	—	0.25	0.11	-0.04
Modern	0.05	0.00	0.08	-0.05	0.04	0.03	0.00	0.11	0.17	0.14	—	0.21	0.09
Expressive	-0.05	-0.06	0.15	0.05	0.00	-0.09	0.05	0.21	0.11	0.14	0.08	—	0.00
Environmentally conscious	0.38	0.42	0.23	0.45	0.32	0.16	0.37	0.21	0.06	0.30	0.38	0.21	—

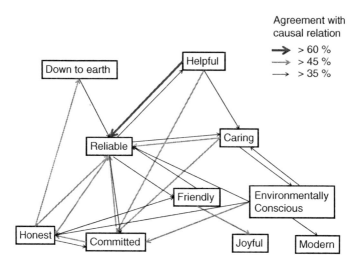

Figure 8.1 How Omo's features cohere

which 'environmental consciousness' is the consequence of the other features does not matter at all: when exploring this relation in a regression analysis, results were far from significant ($\beta = 0.08$, s.d. $= 0.10$, $p = 0.45$, $R^2 = 0.04$). So, even though 'environmental consciousness' has been added later as a feature to Omo, the extent to which it explains the other features is decisive to the extent to which this environmental consciousness comes across as authentic, and not the extent to which it is explained by the other, already existing features. Green claims are thus most convincing if they serve as an *explanans,* not as an *explanandum.*

The key role of causally central features

We have already mentioned above that if a feature is perceived to cause many other features of a brand, people tend to believe that without that feature it is no longer the same brand. Van Rekom *et al.* (2009) showed for four different brands that if a feature has a strong causal role in respondents' thinking about a brand, consumers were indeed inclined to believe that without that feature the brand would no longer be the same. The overall correlation between the extent to which people believed a feature caused all other features of Omo and the extent they believed that Omo would no longer be Omo without that feature should therefore also be strong and significant in our study. This overall correlation was computed by taking the individual respondents' correlations, transforming them into Fisher Z scores, and transforming the average Fisher Z score back into a correlation (Rosenthal 1991). The resulting overall correlation was 0.72 ($p < 0.001$), which is in line with the correlations found by van Rekom *et al.* (2009). The more consumers perceived a feature of Omo to cause Omo's other features, the more they believed Omo would no longer be Omo without that feature. Combining this information with the highly central role Table 8.1 and Figure 8.2 suggest for 'environmentally conscious', we may conclude that this feature has been established quickly and successfully as a core feature in the way consumers think about Omo.

Discussion and implications for managers

This case study set out to investigate the way environmental claims are connected to the personality of a brand. Apparently, it is the degree to which respondents perceived Omo's environmental consciousness to explain its personality characteristics that was significantly related to the degree to which respondents believed Omo's claimed environmental consciousness to be authentic. The method this chapter proposes is useful to investigate consumers' acceptance of green claims made by brands. If consumers indeed – as Holt (2002: 88) puts it so eloquently – 'peel away the brand veneer', they are likely to find environmental consciousness as a factor that to a high extent causes the brand to be what it is, as Table 8.2 and Figure 8.1 show. Environmental consciousness sits at the core of the causal structure which explains how the features of the brand cohere.

Of course, this case study suffers from some weaknesses. Because it was part of a larger study, the online questionnaire became long, and even though we forewarned respondents that the survey would take 25 minutes to respond, only 15 respondents filled in the whole questionnaire. Additionally, the reliance on a snowball sample might not be ideal to get a representative view of the Dutch population, but given the length of the questionnaire, we believed this method to be safer and less prone to self-selection of respondents than more random forms of sample selection. Therefore, this case study should be seen as explorative. Although it is too early to come up with definitive conclusions based upon this case study alone, we believe it to offer a basis for suggestions for further research, and for how management should address concerns for authenticity when introducing claims about their brand being 'green'.

One area of further research that might be worthwhile addressing is the role of brand personality. Since Aaker's (1997) seminal work, this subject has become more and more popular, and intuitively one might tend to believe that brand personality forms a kind of basis for explaining other, more tangible brand manifestations. Our outcomes suggest that this might not necessarily be the case. People may rather rely upon tangible manifestations to explain brand personality, rather than the other way round. And the degree to which they are successful in creating – or believing in – these explanations might be decisive for how authentic they believe these more concrete manifestations are. So one could even wonder as to whether we have been focusing more on brand personality than is warranted by its managerial implications. Whether this is the case, and how this exactly works, is a valuable issue for future research.

Our results suggest important implications for managerial practice. Apparently, if consumers can see features such as environmental consciousness as deeply rooted in the organisation's identity, and if the organisation can explain how its other features derive from it, people may even be more deeply convinced that the green claims made by the organisation are 'real', and that they are not about 'greenwashing', but about 'being green'. Interestingly, it was in particular the extent to which environmental consciousness explained other features which predicted the extent to which Omo's 'environmental consciousness' was perceived to be authentic. This finding is surprising, because Omo became only environmentally conscious at a relatively recent stage of its product life cycle, and has important implications for how organisations should communicate about the green claims of their brand. Apparently, it does not make much sense to explain why a brand has become green as a consequence of other features it already had. On the contrary, it is important that other features can be explained as flowing forth from the brand's green orientation – and this is where the focus of communication around a brand's green positioning may be most fruitful.

References

Aaker, J. (1997) 'Dimensions of brand personality', *Journal of Marketing Research* 34: 347–56.
Ahn, W.-K. (1998) 'Why are different features central for natural kinds and artifacts? The role of causal status in determining feature centrality', *Cognition* 69: 135–78.
Balmer, J. M. T. (2012) 'Corporate brand management imperatives: custodianship, credibility and calibration', *California Management Review* 54(3): 6–33.
Balmer, J. M. T., Fukukawa, K. and Gray, E. R. (2007) 'The nature and management of ethical corporate identity: a commentary on corporate identity, corporate social responsibility and ethics', *Journal of Business Ethics* 76(1): 7–15.
Bears, S., Capozucca, P., Favret, L. and Lynch, B. (2009) *Finding the Green in today's shoppers. Sustainability trends and new shopper insights*, Grocery Manufacturers' Association, Deloitte.
Beverland, M. B. and Farrelly, F. J. (2010) 'The quest for authenticity in consumption: consumers' purposive choice of authentic cues to shape experienced outcomes', *Journal of Consumer Research* 36 (February): 838–56.
Breedveld, K., van den Broek, A., de Haan, J., Harms, L., Huysmans, F. and van Ingen, E. (2006) *'De tijd als spiegel. Hoe Nederlands hun tijd besteden'* [Time as a mirror. How Dutchmen use their time], The Hague: Sociaal Cultureel Planbureau.
Chouinard, Y., Ellison, J. and Ridgeway. R. (2011) 'The sustainable economy', *Harvard Business Review* 89(10): 52–62.
Delmas, M. A. and Cuerel Burbano, V. (2011) 'The drivers of greenwashing', *California Management Review* 54(1): 64–87.
Forehand, M. R. and Grier, S. (2003) 'When is honesty the best policy? The effect of stated company intent on consumer scepticism', *Journal of Consumer Psychology* 13: 349–56.
Holt, D. (2002) 'Why do brands cause trouble? A dialectical theory of consumer culture and branding', *Journal of Consumer Research* 29(June): 70–90.
Karnani, A. (2011) '"Doing well by doing good": the grand illusion', *California Management Review* 53(2): 69–86.
Keil, F. (2006) 'Explanation and understanding', *Annual Review of Psychology* 57: 227–54.

Kent, R. J. and Allen, Ch. T. (1994) 'Competitive inference effects in consumer memory for advertising: the role of brand familiarity', *Journal of Marketing* 58(July): 97–105.

Lai, K., Cheng, T. C. E. and Tang, A. K. Y. (2010) 'Green retailing: factors for success', *California Management Review* 52(2): 6–31.

Parguel, B., Benoît-Moreau, F. and Larceneux, F. (2011) 'How sustainability ratings might deter "Greenwashing": a closer look at ethical corporate communication', *Journal of Business Ethics* 102: 15–28.

Pomering, A. and Johnson, L. W. (2009) 'Advertising corporate social responsibility initiatives to communicate corporate image. Inhibiting scepticism to enhance persuasion', *Corporate Communications, An International Journal* 14(November): 420–39.

Rosenthal, R. (1991) *Meta-analytic procedures for the social sciences*, Applied Social Research Method Series 6, Beverly Hills: Sage.

Schlegelmilch, B. B. and Öbersieder, M. (2010) 'Half a century of marketing ethics: shifting perspectives and emerging trends', *Journal of Business Ethics* 93: 1–19.

Thompson, C. J., Rindfleisch, A. and Arsel, Z. (2006) 'Emotional branding and the strategic value of the doppelganger brand image', *Journal of Marketing* 70(January): 50–64.

Vallaster, Ch., Lindgreen, A. and Maon, F. (2012) 'Strategically leveraging corporate social responsibility: a corporate branding perspective', *California Management Review* 54(3): 34–60.

van Rekom, J., Verlegh, P. W. J. and Slokkers, R. (2009) 'Managing the essence of a brand personality', *Journal of Business Research* 63(3): 181–92.

Vlachos, P. A., Tsamakos, A., Vrechopoulos, A. P. and Avramidis, P. (2009) 'Corporate social responsibility: attributions, loyalty, and the mediating role of trust', *Journal of the Academy of Marketing Science* 37(June): 170–80.

Walker, K. and Wan, Fang (2012) 'The harm of symbolic actions and green-washing: corporate actions and communications on environmental performance and their financial implications', *Journal of Business Ethics* 109(2): 227–42.

9 Haven't we met before?

An investigation into the influence of familiarity on the cognitive processes underlying reputation formation

Simone Mariconda and Francesco Lurati

Introduction

In reputation research, familiarity usually refers to the general level of knowledge that someone has about a certain organisation (Yang 2007). Familiarity with an organisation can be acquired through direct experience of the organisation's product and/or services, hearsay, or media exposure (e.g. Bromley 2000). Researchers have generally agreed that a minimum degree of familiarity is necessary for reputation to form. For instance, van Riel (1997: 298) referred to it as a *conditio sine qua non* for reputation to exist. Other authors have pointed out how '[a] firm's reputation is dependent upon a certain degree of exposure' (Brooks and Highhouse 2006: 107). Similarly, for new organisations, it is critical to become familiar to the public in order to develop a reputation (Aldrich and Fiol 1994; Rindova *et al*. 2007). Indeed, in the absurd case in which nobody knows about an organisation, there would be no reputation.

Most research investigating the relationship between familiarity and reputation has only focused on trying to understand whether or not familiarity is positively related to reputation. As a result of this fairly narrow focus, not much research has sought to understand how familiarity with an organisation might possibly influence perceptions about it. In this chapter, we build on research in social cognition (Fiske and Taylor 1991) to take a step in this direction.

Accordingly, the chapter is structured as follows. First, we begin by briefly reviewing existing research that has investigated the relationship between familiarity and people's impressions. Second, we turn to a discussion of the process of impression formation in order to understand how reputation forms and its relation with familiarity. Third, we conclude by discussing the main findings in relation to two cases representing a familiar organisation and a less familiar one. This discussion will also allow us to identify some implications in the area of corporate communication management.

Familiarity and reputation: a first look

Existing research on the relationship between familiarity and evaluation of an organisation can be divided into two camps: a main one, claiming that familiarity leads to more positive evaluations, and a less prominent one, stating that familiarity plays a more complex role and does not lead a priori only to positive evaluations.

A positive relationship between familiarity and people's attitudes towards organisations has been identified in many different fields, including marketing (Rindfleisch and Inman 1998; Baker 1999), public relations (Yang 2007; McCorkindale 2008), recruitment (Gatewood *et al.* 1993; Turban and Greening 1997; Turban 2001), and corporate reputation (Fombrun and van Riel 2004). In light of such findings, McCorkindale (2008: 395) concluded that 'public relations practitioners should focus on building awareness and knowledge about an organisation'. Similarly, Fombrun and van Riel (2004: 104) concluded 'the more familiar you are to the public, the better the public rates you'.

Research that has found such positive relationship often builds on the notion of the 'mere exposure effect', which refers to the phenomenon according to which the more we are exposed to an object the more we are going to like it (e.g. Zajonc 1968; Bornstein 1989). Research on this effect is 'extensive, detailed and interdisciplinary' (Grimes and Kitchen 2007: 193) and supported by many decades of research in psychology and related disciplines. Principles of mere exposure have been extensively studied in marketing research, suggesting that consumers who had more frequent exposure to a certain brand developed positive affective responses to that brand while simultaneously perceiving it to be more reliable and trustworthy (e.g. Rindfleisch and Inman 1998). For example, Baker (1999) studied how mere exposure can directly influence brand choice, concluding that in some cases mere exposure to a brand may have beneficial effects on consumers by decreasing perceived risk and encouraging brand choice.

Scholars have also provided other reasons explaining why familiarity might lead people to like organisations. For instance, while examining the relationship between students' familiarity with potential employers and attraction towards organisations, Turban (2001) suggested two possible explanations. The first, building on Aaker (1991), claims that people might interpret their familiarity with a certain organisation as a signal of its relevance and quality, thereby ending up liking it more. The second refers to mechanisms of social definition. For instance, Rindfleisch and Inman (1998) claim that more popular brands (and organisations) are seen as being 'socially desirable'; therefore, people display a higher preference for them. Turban (2001), referring to social identity theory (e.g. Ashforth and Mael 1989), suggested that working for a familiar organisation enhances employees' self-definition, making the organisation a more attractive place in their eyes.

Yet the proposition that familiarity leads to liking has been questioned on different grounds. For example, Monin (2003) suggested the existence of a different causal relationship. According to the author, it is not familiarity that leads to liking, but the other way around. Monin coined the expression *Warmth Glow Heuristic* to refer to the warm feeling of familiarity one experiences when presented with pleasant stimuli. Building on this evidence, Brooks and Highhouse (2006: 107) argued that the observation 'that familiarity can both follow from and precede liking suggests that correlational research on firm familiarity and attraction cannot be interpreted in a causal fashion'.

As a result of these and other issues, scholars have started to further investigate the relationship between familiarity and reputation in order to better understand the nature of this relationship. In a series of studies, Brooks and colleagues (Brooks *et al.* 2003; Brooks and Highhouse 2006) found that familiarity is positively related to ambivalence. In fact, because information about familiar organisations – of both a positive and negative nature – is more easily available, people have a higher chance of becoming ambivalent towards such organisations. In one experiment (Brooks *et al.* 2003), students were presented with a list of six pairs of *Fortune 500* companies, with each pair comprising a more familiar firm and a less familiar one. In one condition, students had to choose which one of the companies (one for each of the six couples) was most likely to be fair and honest in dealings and have a supportive corporate culture. The other group instead had to choose which one of the firms (one for each of the six couples) was most likely to be unfair and dishonest in dealings and to have an unsupportive corporate culture. More familiar organisations were more often rated as being simultaneously more fair and honest and more unfair and dishonest. In another study, Gardberg and Fombrun (2002) asked subjects to name the companies with the 'best' and 'worst' reputations. Some of the more often nominated companies for 'best' reputations were often also nominated as 'worst'. The results of these studies can be interpreted by understanding how 'familiarity brings with it a large pool of associations, some favorable and some unfavorable' (Brooks and Highhouse 2006: 108). As such, familiarity was defined as being a 'double-edged sword' (Fombrun and van Riel 2004; Brooks and Highhouse 2006). For similar reasons, Fombrun (1996: 387) talked about the 'burden of celebrity'. We thus understand that the relationship between familiarity and reputation is complex. As mentioned by Brooks *et al.* (2003: 913), 'there is more than meets the eye in the familiarity–reputation connection'.

In the next pages, we investigate the process of impression formation in order to try to understand the different ways in which perceptions are affected by different levels of familiarity with the organisation.

The process of reputation formation: the influence of familiarity

Theories of information processing and impression formation are often the underlying frame of reference for most discussions on the formation of reputation (van Riel and Fombrun 2007). Scholars usually describe the processing of information by breaking it into a series of steps that range from the perception of some kind of stimulus to its interpretation and memorisation (e.g. Engel *et al.* 1990; Fiske and Taylor 1991). Accordingly, we start by looking at the salience of stimuli, one property that makes them more likely to attract attention and thus more likely to be included into reputational judgments; we then discuss how these stimuli are integrated into pre-existing structures and categories in order to be interpreted. As this process is often biased and inaccurate, as third aspect, we discuss some of the most relevant biases and heuristics. The differing levels of familiarity

with the focal organisation, as we will see, play an important role in the information processing, particularly when salient stimuli are included into reputational
judgments.

Properties of stimuli and attention processes: the role of salience

The first step in the formation of an impression is the perception of some kind of
stimulus about an organisation. Such stimuli can include, for instance, direct
contact with a firm's products in a shop, an advertisement on TV, or a newspaper
article describing an organisation's actions (e.g. Sjovall and Talk 2004). Some of
these stimuli are more salient than others and thus more likely to be noticed.
Salience refers to the degree to which certain stimuli stand out relative to others
(e.g. Fiske and Taylor 1991). Specific causes of salience include the extent to
which certain stimuli stand out relative to the perceiver's immediate context, prior
knowledge or expectations, and other attentional tasks (Fiske and Taylor 1991).

Information used for reputational judgments often refers to those characteristics
that are uncommon and/or unexpected (Bromley 1993). Furthermore, according
to research in social judgment and impression formation (Skowronski and
Carlston 1987, 1989) recently applied to the field of organisational reputation
(Mishina *et al.* 2012), there are two types of stimuli that are particularly likely to
stand out relative to people's expectations: positive cues regarding the organisation's ability to achieve results and negative cues regarding the organisation's
inner character. Positive cues signalling a specific capability would be perceived
as being particularly diagnostic of the organisation's abilities and thus more
likely to stand out relative to negative ability cues, which could instead be attributed to the influence of situational factors or lack of motivation. Conversely,
negative cues regarding the particular behavioural characteristics of the organisation (i.e. intentions, dispositions) would be perceived as being more diagnostic
of the true nature of the organisation character and would stand out relative to
positive behaviours, which would instead be considered as the way in which
organisations are normally expected to behave (Mishina *et al.* 2012).

Indeed, the factors that make some of the characteristics of organisations more
salient than others are likely to be common to a large number of people, with the
consequence that there should be some degree of agreement about the organisation's
reputation (Bromley 1993). This might be especially true within homogeneous
stakeholder groups that use similar mental categories to assess organisations (e.g.
Mishina *et al.* 2012). In fact, as we discuss next, these pre-existing frames of reference and categories strongly influence how the perceived stimuli are interpreted.

Categories and attributes in the processes of impression formation

When people encounter new organisations with which they are not familiar,
they associate them with pre-existing frames of reference and categories with
which they are instead familiar (Ashforth and Humphrey 1997; Fischer and
Reuber 2007). This first categorisation requires very little effort, attention,

or motivation; it basically occurs automatically. Fischer and Reuber (2007) pointed out how 'industry' and 'geographical cluster' are the categories in which firms are more likely to be slotted in. These categories may be, for instance, 'internet start-up', 'Italian fashion group', or 'Swiss pharmaceutical'. Organisational and industry reputation are thus strongly interconnected (e.g. Winn *et al.* 2008).

Scholars have defined different relevant aspects related to the categorisation process. Fischer and Reuber (2007) pointed out that the higher the perceived 'entitativity' (i.e. degree of unity, coherence, and consistency) of the category, the higher the probability that people will be assigning stereotyped attributes to the target firm and the higher the level of consensus among different perceivers. Aldrich and Fiol (1994) posited that categorisation of organisations that belong to nascent industries might prove particularly difficult as people are not familiar with such categories and thus lack the adequate frames of reference. Finally, Mahon and Wartick (2003) argued that unfamiliar organisations, when convenient, might purposely exploit the reputation of the category they belong to, using it as a 'surrogate' of their own.

After the first categorisation, the process of impression formation continues only if the focal organisation is relevant to the perceiver (e.g. as a possible investment) and therefore he or she is interested in forming an accurate impression about it. If not, the first categorisation leads to the final impression (Fiske and Neuberg 1990). If interested, the perceiver tries to confirm his or her initial categorisation (confirmatory categorisation). If the attributes analysed in this next stage confirm the initial categorisation, the process ends; otherwise, if there is a certain degree of incongruence between the initial categorisation and the information retrieved in the second stage, a new process of recategorisation takes place. At this point, if the qualities of the target entity are still difficult to fit into any specific pre-existing category, an integration of all the single attributes takes place in order to form a more accurate and personal impression. At this point, category membership will only count as one among the other attributes taken into account to form an impression (Fiske and Neuberg 1990). The more the organisation-specific attributes diverge from those attributed to the category of membership, the more the former gain weight over the latter (Fischer and Reuber 2007).

In this way, impressions are formed through a process that combines categorical inputs, information we already have about the organisation, and specific information we try to find in an attempt to become more familiar with the organisation in which we are interested. This process allows for the formation of complex networks of meanings. In order to deal with this complexity, as we will see in the following section, we use mental shortcuts. Their relevance depends on how familiar we are with the organisation we evaluate.

Mental shortcuts in the process of reputation formation

One of the most recurring themes in management-related discussions is that we do not have the ability to process information in an exhaustive way; we have limited attention and are bounded in our rationality (e.g. Simon 1947). Because of our limited processing abilities and due to the complexity of reality, we rely on mental shortcuts that – while often useful – can also lead to severe and systematic errors (e.g. Taylor 1982). Social judgment biases are likely to influence the process of reputation formation (Mishina *et al.* 2012). As we will see in the conclusive section of this chapter, reputation and corporate communication managers have to be aware of these errors when they make decisions concerning the corporate communication strategy.

Most of these biases have been extensively reported in the social cognition literature. Here we briefly review some of the most important mental shortcuts that influence the process of impression formation and discuss how these cognitive mechanisms are affected by the degree of familiarity with the focal organisation. The first two (i.e. availability heuristic and representativeness heuristic) have to do with the ways in which we form impressions based on probability judgment; the last three (i.e. implicit personality theories, judgment path dependency, and attribution processes) are more related to how we use pre-existing filters when we evaluate objects.

Availability heuristic

This heuristic refers to our tendency to judge the likelihood of a certain event or behaviour based on how quickly and easily examples of it come to mind (e.g. Tversky and Kahneman 1973). It is probably one of the most well-known heuristics used by cognitive psychologists to explain how people make judgments when they do not have full knowledge of the focal objects in which they are interested. It captures the idea, using Ahlstrom and Bruton's (2010: 278) words, that 'if you can think of something, it must be important'. One can easily conclude that the impact of new available information may, *ceteris paribus*, be stronger with people unfamiliar with the organisation who therefore do not have other information available.

The power of this simple mental mechanism is effectively pointed out by Bazerman (2002), who reports how, in an experiment, one of his MBA students made a positive decision based on available information, which – as he later discovered – was negative.

> As a purchasing agent, he had to select one of several possible suppliers. He chose the firm whose name was the most familiar to him. He later found out that the salience of the name resulted from recent adverse publicity concerning the firm's extortion of funds from client companies!
>
> (Bazerman 2002: 16)

The outcome of Bazerman's experiment clearly shows that the mere recollection of the name, regardless of the facts associated with this name, was sufficient to influence his student's decision.

Representativeness heuristic

This heuristic is frequently used when making inferences about the probability of a certain entity (e.g. a person, an organisation) belonging to a certain category (e.g. a profession, an industry). The more the entity is representative of the stereotypical member of a category, the more people will think of it as a member of the category (e.g. Bazerman 2002). As an example, consider the following description of a person: 'Steve is very shy and withdrawn, invariably helpful, but with little interest in people, or in the world of reality. A meek and tidy soul, he has a need for order and structure, and a passion for detail' (Tversky and Kahneman 1974: 1124). Now imagine that, based on this description, you were asked to answer a question about Steve's profession: Is Steve more likely to be a librarian, a farmer, a salesman, an airline pilot, or a surgeon? In this case, using the representativeness heuristic, most people would answer by comparing the description given about Steve to the stereotyped idea of the various professions: Steve is a librarian. 'The representativeness heuristic, then, is basically a relevancy judgment (how well do these attributes of A fit category B?) that produces a probability estimate (how probable is it that A is an instance of category B?)' (Fiske and Taylor 1991: 382). To reiterate, we can say that: 'When judging the probability of an event by representativeness, one compares the essential features of the event to those of the structure from which it originates' (Tversky and Kahneman 1973: 208). When unfamiliar with an organisation, we tend to infer that it belongs to the category of which it is more representative.

Implicit personality theories

We do not limit ourselves to using features to infer to which category an organisation belongs; we also infer additional features of the organisation by using implicit personality theories (IPT). IPT refer to the tendency that we have to immediately infer some characteristics about a certain entity when presented with some of its traits. In a way, we have our own theories of how personality traits are connected to one another; for example, if a person is presented as being intelligent and warm, we may automatically think of that person as also being wise (Asch 1946). The explanation for IPT is that 'traits and traits inferences are embedded in a rich multidimensional structure (…). The structure contains the connections among various traits (e.g. "generous" is close to "sociable" but irrelevant to "intelligent" and contradictory to "selfish")' (Fiske and Taylor 1991: 321). Although developed at the individual level, IPT may be applied to organisations as organisations are commonly perceived as people (e.g. Bromley 1993; Aaker 1997). Vonk and Heuser (1991) studied the relationship between IPT and familiarity and found that people rely on their IPTs only when they have to infer unknown characteristics of a target person. Conversely, when these characteristics are known, they do not need to be inferred.

Judgment path dependency

Social judgment is path-dependent: Impressions, once formed, tend to work as a lens through which we evaluate all subsequent information (e.g. Mishina *et al.* 2012). This pattern might become fairly problematic. In fact, many of our everyday decisions are based on first impressions. As these evaluations are often not reviewed, other decisions involving the same target object are subsequently based on such superficial assessments. One main factor responsible for the perseverance of impressions and beliefs is known as confirmation bias, which refers to the more or less conscious 'seeking or interpreting of evidence in ways that are partial to existing beliefs, expectations, or a hypothesis in hand' (Nickerson 1998: 175). For instance, Hoeken and Renkema (1998) investigated how damages to initial reputation resulting from negative publicity might, in some cases, partially persist even after it is announced that the negative publicity was false or incorrect.

From this we understand how it is critical for organisations to become familiar to the public by making a good impression from the very beginning of their activities or risk being labelled (Ashforth and Humphrey 1997) and/or stigmatised (Devers *et al.* 2009) by being associated, for instance, with a negative event. Once formed, negative reputations might prove particularly sticky and difficult to get rid of (e.g. Fombrun and van Riel 2004). Conversely, if an organisation manages to make a good impression at the outset of its activities, this might help it to navigate through difficult times as a positive reputation will work as an interpretative lens through which new information, even when negative, is filtered (e.g. Rindova 1997).

Attribution processes

When we observe an object – in our case, an organisation – we try to understand its behaviour by inferring causal explanations through what psychologists call attribution processes (e.g. Kelley 1967). However, these processes are affected by what has been observed as our innate tendency to attribute behaviours to internal disposition, a tendency known as fundamental attribution error (Ross 1977).

The fundamental attribution error is '(...) perhaps the most commonly documented bias in social perception' (Fiske and Taylor 1991: 67). When we observe an organisation's actions or read about them in a newspaper, we are more likely to attribute such actions to the organisation's intention rather than to the contextual forces, such as economic factors. Indeed, this tendency seems to be strong even when situational factors are strongly evident. For example, layoffs may be attributed to corporate disposition, even if they occur during a strong economic recession that makes such a decision unavoidable (Sjovall and Talk 2004).

Bromley has argued that the fundamental attribution error seems to be more relevant when the focal object is not familiar:

> The fundamental attribution error (...) is most likely to affect our perception of the people we know least well or know only indirectly through hearsay. Having little or no information about the circumstances affecting the target person's behaviour, and being driven by our 'effort after meaning', we are inclined to attribute their behaviour to internal characteristics, their traits or states of mind. When we make judgments about people we know reasonably well or empathise with, we are more likely to take account of the way situational factors affect their behaviour.
>
> (Bromley 1993: 38)

Therefore distance from the perceived object may influence the likelihood of falling victim to the fundamental attribution error. Thus, stakeholders who are highly familiar with the organisation will be more capable of taking into account the influence of external forces on organisational behaviour and, if it is the case, adjust their opinion of the organisation. However, as we will see in the next section, this may not always be the case.

Familiarity, reputation, and corporate communication: two short case studies

Reputational judgments are triggered by salient stimuli that provide us with the clues necessary to evaluate an organisation (e.g. Bromley 1993). Our level of familiarity with the organisation to which we are exposed, or in which we are interested, plays a central role in the evaluative process. In fact, in the first place it influences the extent to which we are going to rely on attributes we know, through direct experience and vicarious exposure, or on categorical inferences. It then influences the way our mental shortcuts determine the impressions we hold of the focal organisations.

In this final section, we discuss implications of familiarity for the management of reputation by corporate communication (at the end of this section, in Box 9.2, a list of questions that managers should consider is provided). We refer to two cases representing a relatively familiar organisation – Swiss Post – and a relatively less familiar one – Swiss Re (see Box 9.1 for a description of the two organisations). This discussion enables us to foreshadow potential implications for future research.

There are no unfamiliar companies, *tout court.* Companies may be unfamiliar to specific publics, but they will always have publics who have a high level of familiarity with them. Swiss Re, for instance, is not familiar to the general public, but it is extremely well known among its clients, who are by definition a sophisticated public and include risk experts who consider Swiss Re, as we will see, to be a thought-leader in its specific areas of expertise. At the same time, Swiss Post is extremely well known to the general public. Almost all companies and the Swiss population are clients of Swiss Post and have directly experienced its services on almost a daily basis. This familiarity is further enhanced by the long history of the Swiss Post and its iconic status in the Swiss society and landscape. Every remote village in the Swiss Alps used to have a post office and no mountain or country road can be travelled without passing a yellow Swiss Post car. The familiarity of the general public with the Swiss Post is such that even in its business-to-business activities, as we will see, the reputation earned among the private clients has impacted its reputation among the business clients.

Stakeholders' different levels of familiarity with Swiss Re and the Swiss Post influence the cognitive processes that determine their respective reputations. This fact, we will see, corresponds to different patterns of how reputation has formed in the two companies and how they are managing it.

Box 9.1 Description of the organisations featured in the chapter

Swiss Post

Swiss Post is an organisation whose historical roots date back more than 150 years (the federal postal service was first established in 1849). Indeed, the Swiss Post is probably one of the best-known organisations in the country (supported recognition 100 per cent, non-supported 91 per cent) as the company is one of the biggest employers in Switzerland and, more importantly, every Swiss citizen deals with it on an almost daily basis. Swiss Post is active in four markets: communications market, logistics market, retail financial market, and public passenger transport market. Over the years, as a result of the changes in the environment (e.g. market deregulation), Swiss Post has undergone great changes in its organisational structure and services (http://www.swisspost.ch).

Swiss Re

Established in 1863, the Swiss Re Group is one of the world's leading providers of reinsurance, insurance, and other risk-transfer solutions. Because of its industry, the company is relatively unknown to the general public. The company's clients range from insurance firms to other private sector corporations and public sector organisations. Over the years, Swiss Re has managed to develop a very specific reputation among its clients and employees as a knowledge company that actively creates and shares knowledge on issues critical to the development of a resilient society (http://www.swissre.com).

Swiss Re has two stakeholder groups who are extremely familiar with the organisation: its clients and the scientific community. Swiss Re's clients are big organisations, from both the private and public sectors that have generally been with Swiss Re for a long time. Reinsurance is a highly complex and sophisticated business and requires significant interactions between the reinsurer and its clients. These deep relational bonds make attribution processes likely to be more accurate; therefore, the fundamental attribution error is less likely to happen (Bromley 1993) – as was clearly demonstrated during the 2008–2009 events that led then CEO Jacques Aigrain, a former J. P. Morgan Chase & Co. banker, to resign. Following an aggressive and risky investment strategy, Swiss Re incurred major losses unrelated to the traditional insurance business, which led its shares to lose 62 per cent of their value. However, despite this financial meltdown, Swiss Re clients continued to trust the company; senior management's poor management decisions did not affect the strong relationship clients had with the company.

One can argue that they did not attribute the mistakes to the company, but to a trend that unfortunately had hurt numerous companies during those years and hit Swiss Re through the deeds of its CEO, a former investment banker; the *air du temps* was fully recognised as the cause of the crisis, and little or no responsibility was attributed to Swiss Re as a company. This remarkable result was made possible thanks to the outstanding service quality Swiss Re has always provided over the years as well as, as we will see, a sustained effort to provide clients with value that goes beyond the commercial one, thereby creating the conditions for Swiss Re to benefit from the sweet side of the path-dependent judgment mechanism. Swiss Re has positioned itself over the years as a knowledge company, through conferences, seminars, speeches, and concrete projects featuring its core expertise in the diverse areas of risk, including natural catastrophes, population ageing, climate change, aviation, and agriculture. At Swiss Re, people proudly remind you that they are known as the university with a P&L statement, proving the saliency of their activities. Its scientists – ranging from geologists, natural scientists, and mathematicians to psychologists and sociologists – have developed models that help, as they like to say, 'make society more resilient'. Swiss Re believes that its real strength is in its knowledge and its people. Taken together, these elements could be interpreted as manifestations of Swiss Re's core ideology which, using Collins and Porras's words (2000: 221), 'defines the enduring character of an organisation – its self-identity that remains consistent through time and transcends product/market life cycles – technological breakthroughs, management fads, and individual leaders'. The core ideology serves as a guiding element around which relationships (internally and externally) are built and maintained. This is why people come to Swiss Re and why the company is able to differentiate itself not only from its competitors, but also from the financial service industry as a whole. Its strong relationships with clients and the international scientific community are cemented in the knowledge arena, where the core competence of Swiss Re resides. Therefore, its key publics do not need to rely on categorisations to form impressions about the company. This situation put Swiss Re in a comfortable position during the 2008 world financial crisis, when a lack of such a familiarity among its key publics would have most likely led them to form their impressions about the company by relying on availability and representativeness heuristics or IPT – shortcuts that would have trapped Swiss Re's reputation into the financial services one.

Being a highly specialised business, Swiss Re tends to be ignored by stakeholders not directly involved with it. Yet the company remains well aware that this situation may not be permanent. In fact, like any other business, reinsurance is experiencing increasing monitoring and regulations. Making the unfamiliar publics familiar with the company and creating similar bonds to those clients enjoy thus becomes a necessity. Swiss Re does this using the same communication activities it performs for clients and the scientific community. Furthermore, Swiss Re is also heavily engaged in various corporate citizenship activities. For instance, it is considering developing interactive games for schools that allow students to appreciate the concept of risk and its management. Communication efforts have also been made towards special publics, ranging from local communities to regulators. These communication investments may decrease the risk that unfamiliar publics will stereotype the company – a risk that has increased, particularly after the serious financial troubles experienced by the company in 2009; in fact, having been extensively covered by the general media, the chance that availability heuristics will influence perceptions is potentially high (e.g. Brooks *et al.* 2003). Swiss Re sees also a more strategic reason for such investments. Making the general public familiar with the company has beneficial effects in terms of its internally perceived image. As previously mentioned, Swiss Re sees and presents itself as a company where employees not only apply, but also produce knowledge. For this to happen in a sustained way, Swiss Re knows that it is important to maintain pride in the company and therefore motivation. In this respect, fostering the right familiarity around the company can also be considered an important factor (e.g. Turban 2001).

Unlike the Swiss Re case, the general public in Switzerland is quite familiar with the Swiss Post – or at least it seems so at a first look. In fact, while everybody has direct experience with the parcels, letters, and payment services, Swiss Post's corporate communication is still investing heavily in efforts to convey the high-tech and innovative side of its business – the one combining the virtual and real world – through, for instance, electronic mailing and procurement or document services, which are still not very well known by the general public. The general public's perception of Swiss Post is heavily influenced by its history. Because of the dynamics related to judgment path dependency, its reputation has been very stable, ranking very high in credibility, quality and social responsibility, competitiveness, and modernity, although in growth it remains below industry level and its innovativeness is relatively low. The stickiness of this perception is reinforced by availability and representativeness heuristics as well as IPT. In fact, Swiss Post is often associated with other government-owned, or partially owned, companies, such as the Swiss railway system (SBB) and Swisscom, the leading Swiss telecommunication company. Referring to Fischer and Reuber (2007), we can claim that the Swiss general public automatically locates Swiss Post in the public sector category and, consequently, infers stereotypical personality traits due to the high 'entitativity' of the category. We can therefore easily understand the magnitude of the communication challenge Swiss Post has to face in order to change its reputation from a traditional to an innovative company.

It goes without saying that the high level of familiarity Swiss Post enjoys among its different publics is also a source of relevant benefits. Facilitating the dialogue with stakeholders is probably the most important benefit. In 2001, Swiss Post started an optimisation process that, by 2005, had led to the closure of approximately 900 post offices. This project followed the dramatic decrease in its over-the-counter business (43 per cent fewer parcels, 55 per cent fewer letters, and 22 per cent fewer payments in the previous ten years). The changes were clearly imposed by external market factors, such as the replacement of traditional letters with digital communication and other more convenient services, offered by Swiss Post as a response to competition. However, the company had to face strong opposition from the population and its representatives, who felt that it was not living up to its public service mandate. The company was clearly the victim of an attribution error, yet explaining the real reasons behind the painful restructuring project did not work. The public still considered the company responsible. Therefore, Swiss Post decided to change its strategy and engage in intense dialogues, which led to more than a thousand discussions with stakeholders every year. This approach was made possible thanks to its well-established reputation as a credible and socially responsible company and indeed produced remarkable results.

Familiarity is therefore key for understanding why, on the one hand, it is so difficult for Swiss Post to get the public to perceive its new side (Mahon and Mitnick 2010) and why, on the other hand, it has been so successful in carrying out a highly controversial restructuring project, particularly by overcoming unavoidable attribution errors. Swiss Post's image-communication challenge is therefore, as CCO Daniel Mollet says, twofold: overcoming the resilient categorisation made by its publics without destroying it.

The general public plays a central role in Swiss Post's communication strategy. In fact, as previously mentioned, Swiss business clients, when judging the Swiss Post, mostly refer to their own personal experience as private clients and the historical expectations they have towards a socially responsible state-owned company. Swiss Post is quick to point out that 80 per cent of its revenues come from business clients whereas 90 per cent of its reputation comes from private clients. This means that its communication to influence reputation within the business segment also has to go through private clients if it wants to be effective. As long as the private clients perceive Swiss Post as a traditional company with little innovation, the risk is high that business clients will also have the same perception because they are influenced by the availability heuristics coming from their almost daily personal experience with the company as private clients. This additional fact casts further light on the priority private clients have in the image-communication strategy of Swiss Post, despite their already high level of familiarity with the company.

Conclusion

To conclude, in the first part of this chapter, we stressed the fact that familiarity – using Fombrun and van Riel's (2004) expression – is a 'double-edged sword' since it can be the source of ambivalent judgments (Brooks *et al.* 2003; Brooks and Highhouse 2006). In the second part of the chapter, we saw that the lack of familiarity with a company may push publics to evaluate it through categorisations and mental shortcuts. These shortcuts are often the source of evaluative errors. However, as the Swiss Post case study demonstrated, publics may use the same shortcuts to evaluate familiar companies, leading to stable perceptions that may eventually act as obstacles in projecting new (innovative) parts of the company (e.g. Mahon and Mitnick 2010). Thus, familiarity – and not only the lack of it – might have drawbacks; these drawbacks differ from those suggested in earlier literature.

How can we overcome these drawbacks so as to enjoy only the benefits of familiarity? The Swiss Re case may suggest an initial, tentative answer. We have in fact seen that publics familiar with Swiss Re did not use categorisations in judging the company during crisis situations; they stuck with the attributes of the company and did not associate Swiss Re with the broad category of the financial services industry. One could posit that this was possible because Swiss Re managed to create familiarity not around its products, which would link its reputation to the financial services industry, but – as we anticipated – around its own specific core ideology (Collins and Porras 2000).

Can these final results be generalised? Can we claim that familiarity with elements representing a company's core ideology protect the company's reputation better than familiarity with its products and services (e.g. during industry-wide crises)? In particular, would reputation built on familiarity with a company's core ideology decrease the role of categorisations in the process of company judgment?

Box 9.2 Key questions managers should consider in terms of familiarity when managing reputation

- Which publics are (most) familiar with your organisation?
- Are the more familiar publics influencing the other, less familiar, ones? What is their relevance in influencing your overall reputation?
- Are your publics more familiar with the fact that you belong to a certain category (e.g. industry, country) or are they more familiar with the specific characteristics of your organisation?
- To what extent are your publics familiar with your core ideology?
- Does your core ideology highlight what is really specific about your company or is it instead related to the categories to which you belong (e.g. products you sell/your industry)?
- To what extent do you invest in highlighting or downplaying the relationship with your categories of membership (e.g. country, industry)? Does your core ideology help you in doing this?
- Are there any recent contextual events or factors (i.e. not directly related to your organisation) that have gained particular visibility (e.g. through high media coverage) and that can influence how publics evaluate your organisation?
- What are the historical factors regarding your organisation that are particularly well known (to your publics) and that keep influencing your reputation over time (e.g. past achievements or accidents)?
- To what extent is there a risk that your publics blame your company when you make unpopular decisions even if these were influenced by external factors (e.g. economic crisis, market changes)? What are the factors influencing such risk (e.g. historical, industry of belonging)?

In the case that it did, would this also facilitate the generation of new impressions less dependent on the industry of belonging? These are a few questions for potential future research that we hope this chapter has helped identify.

Notes

1 Other terms such as 'visibility', 'prominence', 'awareness', and 'knowledge' have frequently been used as synonyms of familiarity (e.g. Yang and Grunig 2005).
2 A third group worth mentioning, even if not directly relevant for our discussion, sees familiarity and reputation as equivalent – namely, reputation simply consists of being known to the public (see Barnett *et al.* 2006 and Lange *et al.* 2011 for recent reviews on this stream).
3 The two cases were developed by building on two interviews with the CCOs of the two organisations.
4 *Wall Street Journal*, 12 February 2009, 'Swiss Re CEO Aigrain Resigns, Takes Responsibility for Losses', online, available at: http://online.wsj.com/article/SB123440237800775467.html (accessed 17 April 2011).

References

Aaker, D. A. (1991) *Managing Brand Equity: Capitalising on the Value of a Brand Name*, New York: Free Press.
Aaker, J. L. (1997) 'Dimensions of Brand Personality', *Journal of Marketing Research* 34: 347–56.
Ahlstrom, D. and Bruton, G. D. (2010) *International Management: Strategy and Culture in the Emerging World*, Mason, OH: South-Western Cengage Learning.
Aldrich, H. E. and Fiol, C. M. (1994) 'Fools Rush in? The Institutional Context of Industry Creation', *Academy of Management Review* 19(4): 645–70.
Asch, S. (1946) 'Forming Impressions of Personality', *Journal of Abnormal and Social Psychology* 41: 258–90.
Ashforth, B.E. and Mael, F. (1989) 'Social Identity Theory and the Organization', *Academy of Management Review* 14(1): 20–39.
Ashforth, B. E. and Humphrey, R. H. (1997) 'The Ubiquity and Potency of Labelling in Organizations', *Organization Science* 8(1): 43–58.
Baker, W. E. (1999) 'When Can Affective Conditioning and Mere Exposure Directly Influence Brand Choice?', *Journal of Advertising* 28(4): 31–46.
Barnett, M. L., Jermier, J. M. and Lafferty, B. A. (2006) 'Corporate Reputation: The Definitional Landscape', *Corporate Reputation Review* 9(1): 26–38.
Bazerman, M. H. (2002) *Judgment in Managerial Decision Making*, 5th edn, New York: John Wiley and Sons.
Bornstein, R. F. (1989) 'Exposure and Affect: Overview and Meta-analysis of Research', 1968–1987, *Psychological Bulletin* 106(2): 265–88.
Bromley, D. B. (1993) *Reputation, Image and Impression Management*, Chirchester: John Wiley.
—— (2000) 'Psychological Aspects of Corporate Identity, Image and Reputation', *Corporate Reputation Review* 3(3): 240–52.
Brooks, M. E. and Highhouse, S. (2006) 'Familiarity Breeds Ambivalence', *Corporate Reputation Review* 9(2): 105–13.
Brooks, M. E., Highhouse, S., Russell, S. S. and Mohr, D. C. (2003) 'Familiarity, Ambivalence and Firm Reputation: Is Corporate Fame a Double-Edged Sword?', *Journal of Applied Psychology* 88(5): 904–14.

Collins, J. C. and Porras J. I. (2000) *Built to Last. Successful Habits of Visionary Companies*, London: Random House.

Devers, C. E., Dewett, T., Mishina, Y. and Balsito, C. A. (2009) 'A General Theory of Organizational Stigma', *Organization Science* 20(1): 154–71.

Engel, J. F., Blackwell, R. D. and Miniard, P. W. (1990) *Consumer Behavior*, Chicago: Dryden Press.

Fischer, E. and Reuber, R. (2007) 'The Good, the Bad and the Unfamiliar: the Challenges of Reputation Formation Facing New Firms', *Entrepreneurship Theory and Practice* 31(1): 53–75.

Fiske, S. T. and Neuberg, S. L. (1990) 'A Continuum of Impression Formation, from Category-Based to Individuating Processes: Influences of Information and Motivation on Attention and Interpretation', *Advances in Experimental Social Psychology* 23: 1–74.

Fiske, S. T. and Taylor, E. T. (1991) *Social Cognition*, 2nd edn, New York: McGraw-Hill.

Fombrun, C. J. (1996) *Reputation: Realizing Value from the Corporate Image*, Boston: Harvard Business School Press.

Fombrun, C. J. and Shanley, M. (1990) 'What's in a Name? Reputation Building and Corporate Strategy', *Academy of Management Review* 33(2): 233–58.

Fombrun, C. J. and van Riel, C. B. M. (2004) *Fame and Fortune: How Successful Companies Build Winning Reputations*, Upper Saddle River, NJ: Financial Times/ Prentice Hall.

Gardberg, N. A. and Fombrun, C. J. (2002) 'For Better or Worse –The Most Visible American Corporations', *Corporate Reputation Review* 4(4): 385–91.

Gatewood, R. D., Gowan, M. A. and Lautenschlager, G. J. (1993) 'Corporate Image, Recruitment Image, and Initial Job Choice Decisions', *Academy of Management Journal* 36(2): 414–27.

Grimes, A. and Kitchen, P. J. (2007) 'Researching Mere Exposure Effects to Advertising. Theoretical Foundations and Methodological Implications', *International Journal of Market Research* 49(2): 191–219.

Hoeken, H. and Renkema, J. (1998) 'Can Corrections Repair the Damage to a Corporate Image Caused by Negative Publicity?', *Corporate Reputation Review* 2(1): 51–60.

Kelley, H. H. (1967) 'Attribution Theory in Social Psychology', in Levine, D. (ed.) *Nebraska Symposium on Motivation*, Lincoln, NE: University of Nebraska Press.

Lange, D., Lee, P. M. and Day, Y. (2011) 'Organizational Reputation: A Review', *Journal of Management* 37(1): 153–84.

McCorkindale, T. (2008) 'Does Familiarity Breed Contempt? Analyses of the Relationship among Company Reputation, Company Citizenship, and Company Personality on Corporate Equity', *Public Relations Review* 34: 392–5.

Mahon, J. F. and Wartick, S. L. (2003) 'Dealing With Stakeholders: How Reputation, Credibility and Framing Influence the Game', *Corporate Reputation Review* 6(1): 19–35.

Mahon, J. F. and Mitnick, B. M. (2010) 'Reputation Shifting', *Journal of Public Affairs* 10(4): 280–99.

Mishina, Y., Block, E. S. and Mannor, M. J. (2012) 'The Path Dependence of Organizational Reputation: How Social Judgment Influences Assessments of Capability and Character', *Strategic Management Journal* 33(5): 459–77.

Monin, B. (2003) 'The Warmth Glow Heuristics: When Liking Leads to Familiarity', *Journal of Personality and Social Psychology* 85(6): 1035–48.

Nickerson, R. S. (1998) 'Confirmation Bias: a Ubiquitous Phenomenon in Many Guises', *Review of General Psychology* 2(2): 175–220.

Rindfleisch, A. and Inman, J. J. (1998) 'Explaining the Familiarity–Liking Relationship: Mere Exposure, Information Availability, or Social Desirability?', *Marketing Letters* 9(1): 5–19.

Rindova, V. P. (1997) 'The Image Cascade and the Formation of Corporate Reputations', *Corporate Reputation Review* 2(1): 188–94.

Rindova, V. P., Petkova, A. P. and Kotha, S. (2007) 'Standing Out: How New Firms in Emerging Markets Build Reputation', *Strategic Organization* 5(1): 31–70.

Ross, L. (1977) 'The Intuitive Psychologist and his Shortcomings: Distortions in the Attribution Process', in Berkowitz, L. (ed.) *Advances in Experimental Social Psychology*, New York: Academic Press.

Simon, H. A. (1947) *Administrative Behavior*, New York: The Free Press.

Sjovall, A. M. and Talk, A. C. (2004) 'From Actions to Impressions: Cognitive Attribution Theory and the Formation of Corporate Reputation', *Corporate Reputation Review* 7(3): 269–81.

Skowronski, J. J. and Carlston, D. E. (1987) 'Social Judgment and Social Memory: The Role of Cue Diagnosticity in Negativity, Positivity, and Extremity Biases', *Journal of Personality and Social Psychology* 52(4): 689–99.

—— (1989) 'Negativity and Extremity Biases in Impression Formation: A Review of Explanations', *Psychological Bulletin* 105(1): 131–42.

Taylor, S. E. (1982) 'The Availability Bias in Social Perception and Interaction', in Tversky, A., Slovic, P. and Kahneman, D. (eds) *Judgment Under Uncertainty: Heuristics and Biases*, Cambridge: Cambridge University Press.

Turban, D. B. (2001) 'Organizational Attractiveness as an Employer on College Campuses: An Examination of the Applicant Population', *Journal of Vocational Behavior* 58: 293–312.

Turban, D. B. and Greening, D. W. (1997) 'Corporate Social Performance and Organizational Attractiveness to Prospective Employees', *Academy of Management Journal* 40(3): 658–72.

Tversky, A. and Kahneman, D. (1973) 'Availability: A Heuristic for Judging Frequency and Probability', *Cognitive Psychology* 5(2): 207–32.

—— (1974) 'Judgment under Uncertainty: Heuristics and Biases', *Science* 185: 1124–31.

van Riel, C. B. M. (1997) 'Research in Corporate Communication: An Overview of an Emerging Field', *Management Communication Quarterly* 10(1): 288–309.

van Riel, C. B. M. and Fombrun, C. J. (2007) *Essentials of Corporate Communication*, London and New York: Routledge.

Vonk, R. and Heuser, W. J. (1991) 'Implicit Personality Theory and Social Judgment: Effects of Familiarity with a Target Person', *Multivariate Behavioral Research* 26(1): 69–81.

Winn, M. I., Macdonald, P. and Zietsma, C. (2008) 'Managing Industry Reputation: The Dynamic Tension between Collective and Competitive Reputation Management Strategies', *Corporate Reputation Review* 11(1): 35–55.

Yang, S. (2007) 'An Integrated Model for Organization–Public Relational Outcomes, Organizational Reputation, and their Antecedents', *Journal of Public Relations Research* 19(2): 91–121.

Yang, S. and Grunig, J. E. (2005) 'Decomposing Organisational Reputation: The Effects of Organisation–Public Relationship Outcomes on Cognitive Representations of Organisations and Evaluations of Organisational Performance', *Journal of Communication Management* 9(4): 305–25.

Zajonc, R. B. (1968) 'Attitudinal Effects of Mere Exposure', *Journal of Personality and Social Psychology Monograph Supplements* 9: 1–27.

Index

Entries in italic refer to boxes, figures and tables.